In the Shadow of the Throne

Ruth Norrington

In the Shadow of the Throne
THE LADY ARBELLA STUART

PETER OWEN PUBLISHERS
London and Chester Springs

PETER OWEN PUBLISHERS
73 Kenway Road, London SW5 0RE

Peter Owen books are distributed in the USA by
Dufour Editions Inc., Chester Springs, PA 19425-0007

First published in Great Britain 2002 by
Peter Owen Publishers

ISBN 0 7206 1127 X

A catalogue record for this book is available from
the British Library

Printed and bound in India by
Thomson Press (India) Ltd

In memory of the late Dr Ida Macalpine and her son the late Dr Richard Hunter whose brilliant research on porphyria in the Royal House of Stuart inspired me to write this book.

ACKNOWLEDGEMENTS

I should like to thank the following people for their kind assistance in helping me collect the material for this book:

Abbot Dom Richard Yeo and Librarian Dom Daniel Rees for their kindness in letting me use the Monks' Library at Downside Abbey, Stratton-on-the-Fosse, Somerset; the staff of the Bodleian Library, Oxford; the staff of the London Library; the staff of the Tower of London Library; the staff of the Lambeth Palace Library; Len Reilly, Librarian at the Southwick Local Studies Library; the staff of the Guildhall Library, London; Howard Falksohn, Archivist at the Lambeth Archives and the Minet Library; the staff at the London Metropolitan Archives; Gillian White, Curator, and Kath Belshaw, Shop Manager, of Hardwick Hall; Peter Day, Keeper of Collections, and Victoria Edwards, Head of Retail Sales, Chatsworth House; Sue McKenzie, Archivist, Borough of Lambeth; Gwyneth Gosling, Archivist, Literary Institute, Highgate; Dr Kate Harris, Archivist, Longleat House; Robert Harcourt Williams, Librarian and Archivist, Hatfield House; Bridget Clifford, Archivist, Tower of London; Marcia Erikson, North Carolina Museum of Art; Professor John Röhl, University of Sussex; Josephine McKenzie for her research in the Chipping Barnet Library and Barnet Museum; Philip Abbot, Librarian, Royal Armouries, Leeds; and John Barratt, former teacher of history at Clifton College, Bristol, for his help in checking the manuscript. Finally, my late husband Sir Patrick Reilly for his encouragement and research in the Bodleian Library, Oxford.

FOREWORD

In an impressive tomb in the Henry VII Chapel in Westminster Abbey lie three distinguished members of the Royal House of Stuart. They were closely related, all heirs to the English throne and all suffered from the same disease, now believed to be porphyria.

Mary Queen of Scots first became seriously ill with this hereditary disease when she was twenty-four years old, and it was to plague her for the rest of her life. Her grandson, Prince Henry, eldest son of James I, was to die of the illness at the age of eighteen. Lady Arbella Stuart, first cousin once removed to both of them and Mary's niece by marriage, became gravely ill with porphyria in her twenties and died of it in the Tower of London when she was thirty-nine.

In death she lies with the two members of her family who had perhaps been most fond of her: Mary and Henry. Her life, which started with such promise, was blighted by her illness and ultimately destroyed by the implacable anger of her first cousin James I, who never forgave her for marrying William Seymour. James himself was to die of porphyria and lies near her in the chapel of Henry VII.

Today Arbella has sunk into obscurity. My intention in this book is to draw her out of the shadows in which she has languished for so many centuries and place her alongside her illustrious Stuart relatives where she rightfully belongs.

Ruth Norrington

CONTENTS

Foreword   9

List of Illustrations   12

The English Succession to the Throne   13

1. In Her Beginning Was Her End   15

2. 'My Sweet Jewel Arbella'   27

3. Bess's Troublesome Charge   43

4. Prisoner of Hardwick   53

5. The Mystery of Arbella's Behaviour   61

6. The King's Dear Cousin   73

7. First Lady of the Court   87

8. Lady Arbella Seymour   97

9. The House Prisoner   107

10. Escape   119

11. Prisoner in the Tower   135

12. 'What My Birth Did Claim My Death Hath Paid'   143

Epilogue   149

Notes   151

Bibliography   157

Index   161

ILLUSTRATIONS

Between pages 96 and 97

Engraving of Arbella Stuart as a young woman

Portrait of Lord Darnley, aged seventeen, husband of Mary Queen of Scots and father of James I, with his brother Charles Stuart, aged six, who was Arbella's father

The Memorial of Lord Darnley showing James I, the Earl and Countess of Lennox and Arbella's father, Charles Stuart

Elizabeth Talbot, Countess of Shrewsbury (Bess of Hardwick), Arbella's maternal grandmother and guardian, painted in 1581

View of Old Chatsworth House, dated 1680

Lady Margaret Douglas, Countess of Lennox, Arbella's paternal grandmother

Lady Arbella Stuart, aged twenty-three months

Hardwick Hall, Arbella's home until 1603, as it appears today, showing the Ceremonial Staircase and the High Great Chamber

Miniature of Mary Queen of Scots

Sir Walter Mildmay, Elizabeth I's Chancellor of the Exchequer

Lady Arbella Stuart, aged thirteen

Wingfield Manor, Derbyshire, one of the houses belonging to the Shrewsburys where Mary Queen of Scots was held prisoner

Queen Mary's Bower at Chatsworth

James I of England, Arbella's first cousin

James I's wife, Anne of Denmark

Letter from Arbella to Lord Cecil, dated 26 June 1603

Lady Arbella Stuart, painted probably in her mid-thirties

William Seymour, Arbella's husband, later made Duke of Somerset by Charles II

Sir Theodore Turquet de Mayerne, James I's physician

Prince Henry, King James's eldest son

Letter from Arbella to the Lords Chief Justice, March 1610, revealing her distress at being separated from her husband

The chamber in the Bell Tower of the Tower of London where Arbella is said to have been kept prisoner until her death

Lady Arbella Stuart's burial place, which she shares with Mary Queen of Scots and Prince Henry in Henry VII's Chapel, Westminster Abbey

THE ENGLISH SUCCESSION TO THE THRONE

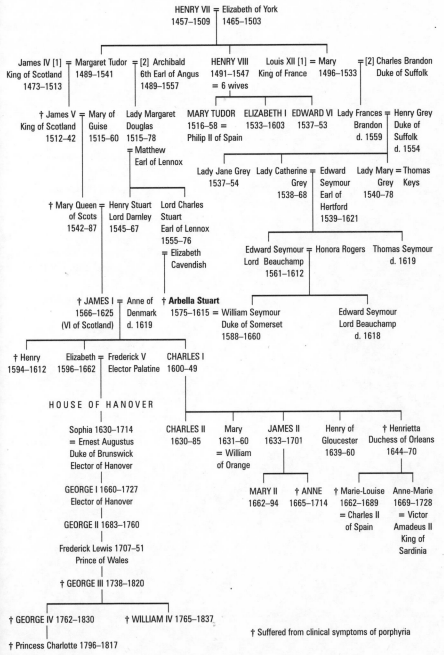

† Suffered from clinical symptoms of porphyria

1

IN HER BEGINNING WAS HER END

In 1575, at Chatsworth House in Derbyshire, a baby girl was born to Bess of Hardwick's daughter, the young Countess of Lennox, formerly Elizabeth Cavendish. The child's pedigree was impressive. She was the great-great-granddaughter of Henry VII, great-granddaughter of Henry VIII's elder sister Margaret Tudor and first cousin once removed to Mary Queen of Scots and her niece by marriage. She was also first cousin to James VI of Scotland, first cousin once removed to Elizabeth I, niece of the ill-fated Lord Darnley and first cousin once removed to Lady Jane Grey and her sister Catherine. The significance of this lineage was to dog her life from her cradle at Chatsworth to her deathbed in the Tower of London.

It was her formidable grandmother, Bess of Hardwick, Countess of Shrewsbury, who was the most significant person in her life when she was young; certainly she was to drive Arbella almost to distraction in her late teens and early twenties. Bess and her fourth husband, the Earl of Shrewsbury, had been gaoler to Mary Queen of Scots for six years at the time of Arbella's birth, a role that seemed to come naturally to Bess and one which she adopted with fateful consequences with her granddaughter.

In spite of six marriages Henry VIII had no grandchildren to perpetuate the Tudor dynasty when his children died. The absence of obvious heirs was to dominate the lives of those who were born close to the throne, whether they wished to succeed to it or not. Poor Arbella was, with her cousin James VI, the closest heir and therefore the most vulnerable.

Henry VIII's second child, Elizabeth, was the first monarch after Henry to be faced with the dilemma of succession, and she fell back on her habit of shelving difficult problems in the hope that they would resolve themselves whenever the issue was raised. It was only a nod of the head of the dying Queen that gave James VI the throne, even though many people thought that Arbella, who had been born on English soil, had the better claim.

Two branches of descendants laid claim to the throne through Henry VII. The elder branch descended from his elder daughter, Margaret, and the younger branch from his younger daughter, Mary. Margaret Tudor married James IV of Scotland in 1503. She had one son by him, before he was killed at the Battle of Flodden in 1513. Soon afterwards, in 1514, she married the handsome Archibald Douglas, sixth Earl of Angus. At the time of their marriage she was reluctantly forced to give up the regency for her young son, James V. She later escaped to England to give birth to a daughter by her second marriage, also named Margaret.

Margaret Douglas did not get on well with her mother but adored her father, and when her parents were divorced she was sent to the court of her uncle Henry VIII, under the protection of his younger sister Mary, Duchess of Suffolk. When Mary died she was transferred into the care of his eldest child, the Princess Mary, who was still in favour at the time. After Henry divorced Catherine of Aragon and married Anne Boleyn he sent for Margaret to be first lady of honour to the baby Elizabeth. After Anne Boleyn's execution Elizabeth was pronounced illegitimate, as her sister Mary had been after Henry's divorce from Catherine, thus making Margaret heir presumptive to the throne. But by this time the Alien Act had been passed, barring anyone not born on English soil from inheriting lands and property in England or succeeding to the English throne.

Margaret Douglas was a typical Tudor, hot-blooded and wilful, and she chose the moment when she was in high favour with Henry as his heir to fall in love with the young Lord Thomas Howard, younger brother of the Duke of Norfolk and kinsman to Anne Boleyn, who, before her fall from grace, had secretly encouraged the young lovers. However, Henry was appalled when he heard of the entanglement and had them both incarcerated in the Tower of London.

An Act of Attainder was bought against Howard which stated, 'That any man of what estate and condition so he be, who shall hereafter take upon him to espouse, marry or take to his wife any lady of the Royal Family without the King's consent under the great seal, shall be held guilty of high treason, and the woman so offending equally so, and subject to the same punishment.'[1] This would appear to be the first known

Royal Marriage Act. Its dire consequences were later to have a devastating effect on Margaret Douglas's granddaughter, Arbella Stuart.

Margaret and her lover languished in the Tower during the summer of 1536. Both fell victim to the fever that was prevalent there and which caused the death of many of its inhabitants. In November the King took pity on Margaret and removed her to the Sion Convent on the Thames. After the birth of his son Edward she was finally released and allowed to return to court. No such leniency was extended to Howard, and he died of fever in the Tower in 1537.

Although Margaret had several more love affairs, including one with the nephew of Lord Thomas, her earlier experiences had taught her a lesson, and she did not marry until she was nearly thirty. Her spouse, chosen by the King, was Matthew Stuart, fourth Earl of Lennox. Although this was a marriage of convenience, the pair were very happy together. Of their eight children, only two survived; the eldest son, Lord Darnley, who was to marry Mary Queen of Scots, and Charles Stuart, father of Arbella.

Mary had become Queen of Scotland when she was just a week old. Betrothed to Francis, the Dauphin of France, she was sent to the French court when she was six and was educated there with the royal children. In 1558, at the age of sixteen, she was married to Francis. That year Mary I died. She had come to the English throne in 1553 after her brother Edward VI died.

The Dauphiness's father-in-law, Francis I, took the unwise step of proclaiming Mary Queen of Scots 'Queen of England, Ireland and Scotland' and made the young Dauphin and Dauphiness assume the royal arms of England as well as those of France and Scotland. Unable to protest – even if she had wished to do so – the young Mary thus fatally enraged her cousin Elizabeth, who never forgave her for her presumption, which was to be brought up at her trial thirty years later.

In 1560 Mary's ailing husband, by then Francis II, died, and in 1561 the young widowed Queen returned to Scotland. The Earl and Countess of Lennox were soon making plans for a possible marriage between her and their eldest son, Lord Darnley. News of this reached Queen Elizabeth, and they were summoned to London. The Earl was placed in the Tower and his wife in the custody of Sir Richard and Lady Sackville at Sheen. After many letters from the Countess to William Cecil, Lord Burghley, her husband was allowed to join her at Sheen in 1562; by this time he was very ill, probably as a result of his sojourn in the Tower. In 1563 they were granted their freedom and allowed to return to their house at Settrington, Yorkshire, but were not taken back into the royal favour. They were ruined financially by the imprisonment but were determined to advance their son's marriage to Queen Mary.

The Earl and Lord Darnley went to Scotland to meet Mary, leaving the Countess at home with the younger brother, Charles. Although Darnley was three years younger than Mary and an idle fop, he was good-looking and extremely tall. In fact he was one of the few men Mary had met who was taller than herself, as she was over six feet in height, then extremely unusual in a woman. His appearance, not to mention his proximity to the English throne, endeared him to her, and in 1565 they were married. Unable to vent her wrath on the absent Earl, Elizabeth summoned Margaret to London, stripped the Earl of his property and imprisoned the Countess in the Lieutenant's Lodgings in the Tower of London. She was comfortable there but desperately anxious about the absence of her husband and the enforced separation from her young son, Charles, who had been left behind at Settrington with a few servants to take care of him.

Elizabeth herself was worried about her young kinsman, fearing that he might also be spirited away to Scotland, and she sent Charles Vaughan and his wife Lady Kynevet to take charge of the young boy at Settrington.[2] In 1566 Mary and Darnley had a son, the future James VI, but the following year Darnley was murdered at Kirk O'Field. His parents were devastated and accused their daughter-in-law of complicity in the murder. Elizabeth, witnessing their grief and anger, allowed the Countess and the Earl to return to their young son at Settrington. They found he had developed severe behavioural problems and that his education had been badly neglected.

After her disastrous third marriage to the Earl of Bothwell and defeat at the Battle of Langside, Mary abdicated in favour of her baby son, James, who was put in the care of the Earl of Mar, and fled to England in 1568. Elizabeth was shocked at the rage of the Lennox family against Mary. She was placed in the custody of the Earl of Shrewsbury, and the Earl of Lennox was made Regent for his young grandson, James, and returned to Scotland. Further tragedy struck the family in 1572, when the Earl of Lennox was murdered at Stirling. His successor as Regent, the Earl of Mar, conferred the Earldom of Lennox on his son, Charles, for himself and his heirs unconditionally. Elizabeth was happy about this and wrote to thank him for his consideration of her young kinsman.

Margaret was grief-stricken at her husband's death and extremely anxious about the welfare of her young son. She decided to move into a property of the Earl's in Hackney, which he had gained from the disgraced Percy family while he was in Scotland. Here the boy was at last put in the charge of a good tutor called Malliet, and during the two years they were together he improved out of all recognition. Elizabeth wanted the boy to be bought up Protestant, and the Roman Catholic Countess agreed to this. 'The youth is just entering on his sixteenth year,' wrote Malliet, 'and gives great promise of hope for the future. For in case the present King should die without lawful issue he is the sole successor by hereditary right to the Crown of Scotland and is entitled to be placed at the head of the kingdom and empire. So also no one is more nearly allied to the royal blood after the death of the present Queen than his mother, to whom her only son is heir.'[3]

The two comparatively peaceful and constructive years that Charles spent with his mother and tutor in Hackney were bought to an end by her secret plans for his marriage to the Earl of Shrewsbury's stepdaughter, Elizabeth Cavendish, whose mother, Bess of Hardwick, shared her husband's duties as Mary's gaoler.

Bess was the fourth daughter and co-heiress of John Hardwick of Hardwick Hall in Derbyshire. Her first marriage had been to Robert Barlow, a rich young landowner besotted with her; he was a chronic invalid, and Bess made herself responsible for his care, including his diet and his medicines, and generally became indispensable to him. He died in 1533, a year after their marriage, leaving her all his property. Her second husband, the love of her life, was Sir William Cavendish. She met him when she was lady-in-waiting to Frances Grey, Marchioness of Dorset, Duchess of Suffolk and mother of Lady Jane Grey. He was a clever statesman, whose eldest brother was George Cavendish who wrote the brilliant life of Cardinal Wolsey. In 1530 William had visited the monasteries to arrange the surrender of their property, and he acquired at this time the Abbey of Sheen. In 1541, as Auditor of the Court of Augmentations, he received grants of lands in Hertfordshire. By 1546 he was Treasurer of the King's Chamber, knighted and sworn as a member of the Privy Council. Henry remained devoted to him, and

Edward VI, after Henry's death, continued to favour him and increased his landed property.

William Cavendish's first wife was Margaret Bostock, who gave him two daughters and died in 1540. He married a second time in 1542 to Elizabeth Parker who died childless. Bess of Hardwick, whom he married in 1549, was thus his third wife and he was her second husband. He adored her and could refuse the acquisitive Bess nothing – to the detriment of his first family. He had eight children by her, of whom six survived to be powerful people in their own right, exploiting their position later on as stepchildren of the Earl of Shrewsbury, Bess's fourth husband.

William Cavendish's main property was in the south of England, but on his marriage he sold it and bought Chatsworth from his wife's family. It came into their possession through the second marriage of Bess's mother, Elizabeth, to Ralph Leche, a younger son of the owners of Chatsworth. Bess's younger sister, Alice, married Francis Leche, son of her stepfather's eldest brother, who had inherited the estate. Finding themselves unable to maintain it, they sold it to Frances Agard, who was also unable to pay for its upkeep. He sold the house and land to Sir William Cavendish for £600. It was purchased in the joint names of William and Bess. For their stays in London the Cavendishes moved into an imposing house in Chelsea, where they entertained lavishly many of their Derbyshire friends. While Bess was in London her mother and sister took charge of affairs at Chatsworth, and large quantities of furnishings, tapestries and plate were sent there from the city. After Mary Tudor came to the throne the Cavendishes spent most of their time in Derbyshire. Cavendish, who was the Queen's Treasurer, got into tax difficulties and fell ill on one of his visits to London. Bess hastened there to be with him. To her great grief he died on 25 October 1557.

She sold the London house, but on Mary Tudor's death in 1558 returned to court as lady-in-waiting to Queen Elizabeth. Here she met her third husband, Sir William Saintlow. He was another very wealthy landowner, Captain of the Guard to Queen Elizabeth and Grand Butler of England, and they married in 1559. He had a daughter by a previous marriage, but she, like Bess's previous two stepdaughters, was to be deprived of her inheritance by her avaricious stepmother who persuaded her third husband to leave all his property to her and her offspring. He agreed to support Bess's children, paying for the sons' education at Eton, and gave a handsome dowry to her daughter. He also supplied Bess with huge sums of money to rebuild Chatsworth and paid off Sir William's debt of £1,000. He spent as much time as possible at the estate, which he loved, and would fondly refer to his wife as 'his dear Chatsworth'. When Bess was made Lady of the Bedchamber to the Queen, the couple spent a considerable amount of time at court together. It was during this period that Bess would have come to know Margaret Lennox.

Saintlow was devoted to Bess and, like her previous husbands, made a will leaving her most of his possessions. He was a delicate man who died in 1565 after only six years of marriage. Bess continued to spend time at court, where she met George Talbot, sixth Earl of Shrewsbury. A widower, he had six children by a previous wife, and he, too, was captivated by Bess.

Bess seems to have fascinated so many people that she must have possessed considerable charisma and beauty. She was quite tall, with ash-blonde hair, hazel eyes and slim and elegant hands. She was generous to her dependants, entertained lavishly and was known as a lively conversationalist.

Bess's main aim in life was to marry off her children to wealth and power, and she made it a condition of marriage to George Talbot that he agree that her daughter Mary marry Gilbert Talbot, George's second son, who inherited the earldom on his father's death and that Bess's eldest son, Henry Cavendish, marry the Earl's daughter Grace. Henry and Grace were childless, but he had an illegitimate son – the ancestor of the present Lord Waterpark.

Bess's second and favourite son, William Cavendish, who later became the first Earl of Devonshire, was bought up with his stepbrothers and sisters, although he was to get on badly with them in later life. Her third son, Charles, married Catherine Ogle, and their son William became the first Duke of Newcastle. Another daughter, Frances, married Sir Henry Pierrepoint of Nottingham, one of the many noble families who harboured the Jesuit Edmund Campion on his journeys in that part of England, and she was an ancestor of the Duke of Kingston.

When Margaret Lennox was looking for a wife for her son Charles, Bess was searching for a husband for her remaining unmarried daughter Elizabeth. The two powerful women secretly discussed a marriage apparently advantageous to them both. For Bess, a marriage of her daughter to a man so close to the throne not only of England but of Scotland would be a brilliant match. Margaret Lennox was equally delighted with the prospect of a marriage that would confirm her son's proximity to the throne and also bring great wealth into the family. Although both mothers were well aware of how greatly the Queen would disapprove of a marriage between two near relatives of hers without her express permission, they laid their plans carefully for a meeting between the two young people.

The prospective bride was a charming and gentle girl who had spent much of her childhood in the company of her stepfather's prisoner Mary Queen of Scots. Mary, who had been denied the company and comfort of her son James, was delighted to have the little girl as a companion and made a great fuss of her during the long days of her captivity. Mary had been deeply upset by the false accusations made against her by the Lennox family, namely that she had been responsible for the death of their son Darnley, and she saw a marriage between her young brother-in-law Charles and the delightful Elizabeth Cavendish as a chance to heal the breach between them. The marriage was discussed at great length between Mary and Bess of Hardwick.

Margaret decided that it was time she went up to see her home at Settrington and continue her journey to Scotland to visit her grandson, now James VI, taking her son Charles with her. She planned to stay *en route* with her niece Katherine, Duchess of Suffolk, now married to a Mr Bartie, at Huntingdon. During an interview with the Queen before her departure, she was forbidden to go to Sheffield or Chatsworth, where she might have encountered Mary Queen of Scots.

However, the wily Bess of Hardwick was more than a match for the Queen, and she decided to take her pretty daughter to Rufford, one of her many properties not far from the house at Huntingdon where Margaret and her son Charles were staying. Bess contacted them there and offered to meet them on the road when they left Huntingdon and take them to stay at Rufford. On arrival Margaret conveniently succumbed to an illness and took to her bed for five days, apparently long enough for the young couple to fall in love. Margaret, in a letter written later defending her behaviour, wrote, 'Rufford was not one mile distant out of my way, yea a much fairer way, as is well to be proved, and my Lady meeting me herself upon the way, I could not refuse it, being near thirty miles from Sheffield.'[4]

Charles fell so deeply in love with Elizabeth that he swore he would have no other bride. Elizabeth's unhappy stepfather, the Earl of Shrewsbury, wrote in haste to the Earl of Leicester on 5 November, probably after the wedding, to exonerate himself from any complicity in the affair. 'The young people have so tied themselves upon their own liking as cannot part. My wife hath sent him to my lady [of Lennox] and the young man is so far in love that belike he is sick without her. There are few noblemen in England that [my wife] has not prayed me to deal for at one time or another . . . and now this comes unlooked for without thanks to me.'[5]

The spectacular success of the plans of these two redoubtable mothers caused the journey north to be abandoned and the marriage rushed though, and by the beginning of November Charles and Elizabeth were husband and wife. By 17 November the news had reached the ears of the Queen, and great was her wrath that such a marriage should have taken place without her consent, even though this was to heal the breach between Mary Queen of Scots and the Lennox family caused by Darnley's murder. Elizabeth immediately summoned all the parties concerned to London, and the wretched young bride and groom and the two mothers set out on the arduous journey south in appalling weather.

Shrewsbury was alarmed by the situation and sent a letter, via the Earl of Leicester and Burghley, to Queen Elizabeth trying to dissociate himself for his headstrong wife's behaviour.

I must confess, Your Majesty, as true it is, that it was dealt in suddenly and without my knowledge; but as I dare undertake and assure to your Majesty, for my wife, she finding her daughter disappointed of young Barte, where she hoped, and that the other young gentleman was inclined to love with a few days' acquaintance, did her best to further her daughter to this match, without therein having any other intent or respect than with reverent duty towards your Majesty she ought. I wrote of this matter to my good Lord of Leicester a good while ago, at great length. I hid nothing from him that I knew was done about the same; and thought not meet to trouble Your Majesty therewith, because I took it to be of no such importance as to write of, until now that I am urged by such as I see will not forbear to devise and speak what may procure any suspicion or doubtfulness of my service here.'[6]

The Earl wrote from Sheffield where he was with Mary Queen of Scots. He feared for his position as her gaoler in this family crisis. By 3 December the non-arrival in London of the offending parties was causing great concern. In fact they were trapped in Huntingdon by floods and would not arrive in London until 10 December.

Margaret Lennox and the bride and groom were escorted to the house in Hackney under arrest and Bess of Hardwick was taken to her husband's house. After Christmas the two women were summoned to the Tower, and as Margaret Lennox entered the dismal place she ruefully commented that this was the third time she had been sent there over love matters.

Under a Commission set up by the Earl of Huntingdon, Thomas Fowler, the trusted steward of Margaret Lennox, was closely questioned about the affair, together with the rest of the household, but no plot was discovered and the secret of the planned marriage was well kept. The two mothers were released from the Tower in March. Bess returned to her house at Sheffield, and from there she went to Buxton to recover her health. Margaret Lennox, with her son and new daughter-in-law, returned to the house in Hackney. By this time the bride was pregnant, and she and her husband returned to Chatsworth to await the birth of a much-hoped-for son. To their great disappointment the young Countess of Lennox gave birth to a girl in September 1575.

Under the Alien Act, no one born out of England could inherit the throne; therefore great care was taken to ensure that the child was born on English soil. Had the baby been a boy, there is little doubt that he would have been recognized by Elizabeth as having a stronger claim to the throne than James. However, the infant was a girl, and she was christened Arbella, probably in the little parish church of Endesor next to Chatsworth where all Cavendish religious ceremonies were performed. Charles Cavendish, one of her mother's brothers, was one godparent and his sister Mary, married to Gilbert Talbot who became Earl of Shrewsbury, was another. She was to be a loyal friend and confidante to Arbella all her life. There are two references to Arbella's birth in the Harleian Manuscripts: 'Arbella nata 1575 apud Chatsworth in Anglia'; Chatsworth is written in different ink from the rest of the documents and obviously added after the birthplace had been confirmed.[7]

The long-standing feud that had existed between the Lennox family and Mary ended with her birth. A letter dated 10 November, written by

Margaret Lennox to her daughter-in-law, shows that they were on excellent terms once more. She thanks her for her 'good remembrance and bounty to her little granddaughter, who some day may serve your Highness' and signs herself 'Your Majesty's most humble and loving mother and aunt'. Elizabeth has added a note to the letter thanking her for her remembering her poor servant both with a token and in her gracious letter.[8]

Mary Queen of Scots immediately took a great personal interest in her and lavished much attention on her, and there was no reason to suppose that Arbella should not have brothers and sisters in due course. But before she was a year old her young father, Charles, died of consumption in April 1576. His death plunged his widow and child from a situation of great wealth and security into near poverty. When Matthew, the father of Lord Darnley and Charles Stuart, died, his title of Earl of Lennox reverted to James VI as his grandson. But in April 1572 James granted the Earldom to Charles Stuart and his heirs. By the time of Charles's death James was a grasping boy of ten sheltering behind the late Regent. He allowed the new Regent, Lord Morton, to disinherit the fatherless Arbella, leaving her mother dowerless. The Regent, it was stated, was 'requested to grant the wardship of the lands unto Elizabeth, Countess of Lennox for her dower, not only denied the same but also denied to allow the Lady Arbella as heir to the Earldom. So that the Regent will not permit the Countess to deal with the said Earldom neither in her own right as her dower, nor the right of the young lady as tutor or guardian to her.'[9]

Such an injustice was to spark a long controversy over her title which dogged her life for years. It darkened the last days of old Margaret Lennox's life and perhaps shortened that of her daughter Elizabeth. Margaret wrote to Lord Ruthven in April 1576 regarding her granddaughter's claim to the title and lands but in vain. Queen Elizabeth and Lord Burghley took up the cudgels on Arbella's behalf but also with no success. Morton was adamant. The Earldom had fallen into the hands of King James by reason of ward on Charles's death, and Arbella's claims would not be considered until she was eighteen years old. He also stated that any gift made by the Regent during the King's minority might be revoked by the Sovereign at any time 'either within age or at full age'.[10]

'MY SWEET JEWEL ARBELLA'

In November 1575 Arbella and her parents went to Hackney to stay with the old Countess of Lennox. After her father's death in April the following year the young widow and her daughter, while still spending some time at Hackney and sometimes visiting her aunt and uncle, Mary and Gilbert Talbot, lived mostly in one or other of the palatial homes belonging to Bess of Hardwick: Chatsworth, Wingfield, Sheffield and Hardwick. It was thus that Mary Queen of Scots got to know and love her little niece and did all she could – which was little enough in her position – to assure her just inheritance.

The intelligent little girl must have wondered at the strange circumstances in which the Queen of Scots lived. Mary's grief and rage at her situation – and the ill health that accompanied this – must have had a profound effect on the impressionable child. Years later, when Arbella found herself a virtual prisoner of Bess, memories must have been stirred in her of her tragic aunt. In many ways Arbella's sometimes irrational behaviour was reminiscent of Mary's. Indeed, the latter's recurrent bouts of ill health have now been diagnosed as porphyria, and her symptoms bear a striking resemblance to ones that Arbella would experience many years later.

Arbella's cousin Elizabeth Pierrepoint joined Mary's household in 1572 at the age of four. She was the daughter of Bess's daughter Frances, who had married Sir Henry Pierrepoint. Mary was besotted with this charming little girl. Unfortunately she was to turn into a haughty, rather unattractive woman who would marry the equally unappealing Thomas Erskine, Viscount Fenton, when she was thirty-five. As a child, however, she shared Mary's bed and was treated like her daughter; Mary even made clothes for her.

There was seven years' difference in age between the two girls, and the friendship which began with their romps in the vicinity of the imprisoned Queen was to last until Arbella's death. In the early days of her childhood Arbella was treated with great deference, and no effort was spared for her education and comfort. The child grew accustomed to being treated as royalty and became very spoilt, which made it hard for her to adjust when her grandmother's attitude towards her changed dramatically later on. Her aunts and uncles made a great fuss of her, and the many visitors who came to visit the Shrewsburys and Queen Mary were always presented to Arbella as well. Robert Beale, a clerk to the Privy Council and great friend of the Earl, always referred to her as 'my little Lady Favour', and Sir Walter Mildmay also mentioned meeting her. Writing to his brother-in-law, Walsingham, from Hardwick on 17 June 1583, he said:

> After the closing of my letter to you, I received this little enclosed paper written with the hand of Lady Arbella, daughter of the late Earl of Lennox. She is about seven years old and learned, this Christmas last. A very proper child and, to my way of thinking, will be like her grandmother, my old Lady Lennox. She wrote this at my request, and I meant to have shown the same to her Majesty and withal to have presented her humble duty to her Majesty with her with her daily prayer for her Majesty, for so the little lady desired me. And now by reason of my not coming this time to her Majesty's presence, I shall pray you to do this which I should have done.[1]

Bess and Mary would sit for hours working on exquisite embroidery, some examples of which can be seen today at Hardwick Hall and at Oxborough Hall in Norfolk. Arbella's lifelong love of embroidering, which kept her occupied through so many lonely hours, would certainly have developed at this time. However, Queen Mary's growing hostility to Bess arose partly because the latter made it increasingly apparent that she and her family regarded Arbella as Queen Elizabeth's rightful heir, not her son James of Scotland, and partly because of Bess's scurrilous accusations that Mary was having an affair with her husband – which she hotly denied.

Nevertheless, in spite of her extraordinary circumstances, aggravated by the deteriorating relationship between Bess and her husband, Arbella was much loved by her relatives and was allowed to spend a good deal of time in rural pursuits as well as in study. Her paternal grandmother, the old Countess of Lennox, died at Hackney on 9 March

1578, when Arbella was nearly three. She left huge debts behind her and no money to pay them. Queen Elizabeth, not wishing to draw attention to the fact that such a close relative had not left enough money to pay for her funeral – largely owing to the fact that the Queen had sequestered her inheritance – paid for a grand state funeral at Westminster Abbey, and the Countess, too, now lies in an elaborate tomb in the Henry VII Chapel. The one thing she could bequeath her granddaughter was a casket of jewels, which contained some remarkable pieces. The list is of considerable interest:

1. A jewel set with a fair table diamond, a table ruby and an emerald with a fair great pearl.
2. A cross set with fair table diamonds, with a square linked chain.
3. A jewel set with ballast, and a fair table diamond set beneath it.
4. An H of gold set with rock ruby.
5. A burrish set with a fair diamond.
6. A rose set with a fair diamond.
7. A carcanet [necklace] set with table diamonds.
8. A girdle set with table diamonds.
9. A border [head-band] set with table diamonds.
10. A border set with table rubies.
11. A border set with rock emeralds.
12. A table [ring] the head of gold set with diamonds.
13. A fair pearl chain.
14. A chain set with rock rubies pillar-wise.
15. A chain of small turquoise set upon a three square pillar.
16. A clock set in crystal, with a wolf of gold upon it.
17. Buttons of rock rubies to set a gown.
18. Table diamonds to set upon sleeves.
19. Two tablets of gold, the one with two agates, with divers small turquoises the other.
20. Enamelled the form of a globe.
21. Bracelets two pair; one of agate, the other of plain gold, with other things that be not yet in memory.[2]

Arbella was supposed to have been given this remarkable inheritance when she was fourteen, but the casket was handed for safe keeping to the Countess's trusted servant, Thomas Fowler, who, after his mistress's death, went up to Scotland to serve James, taking it with him. Mary Queen of Scots tried to prevent this by decreeing that the casket should be handed into the care of Bess of Hardwick at Chatsworth, but, like most of Arbella's possessions, the jewellery never reached her. It was stolen by the Earl of Bothwell in a raid in Scotland. On being recovered, James took safe custody of it and later, to help pay off his debts, handed the collection over to money-lenders.

Mary wrote to Beaton, Archbishop of Glasgow, her Ambassador in France, with news of her mother-in-law's death, confirming the excellent relationship between them and hinting at the threat that Arbella might pose to her inheriting the English throne. She wrote, 'May, 1578. The Countess of Lennox, my mother-in-law, died about a month ago, and the Queen of England has taken into her care her ladyship's granddaughter [Arbella Stuart]. I would desire those who are about my son to make instances in his name for this succession, not for any desire that I have that he should actually succeed to it, but rather to testify that neither he nor I are to be reputed or treated as foreigners in England, who are both born within the same isle.'[3]

In a letter to William Cecil in January 1564, some years before her death, the Countess had described the symptoms of an illness she had experienced – very similar to the symptoms of an ailment suffered later by Mary Queen of Scots, James Stuart and Arbella. The historian Agnes Strickland, commenting on this letter, wrote, 'She acknowledges as constitutional the same malady which subsequently proved fatal to her, thus exonerating any accounts of poisoning her. She had James V in mind, her son, and father of Mary Queen of Scots, who had similar symptoms.'[4]

The wrangling between Elizabeth and James over the Lennox English and Scottish estates went on, and James sent an envoy, the Abbot of Dunfermline, to Elizabeth in 1578 to discuss the disputed English properties. It was the failure of these discussions that led James to fear that his cousin Arbella might, in English law, have a better right to them and the English throne than he did. She was, after all, born on English soil, while he was considered a foreigner and therefore unable to inherit any property in England.

Still too young to be aware of what was going on, Arbella was thus deprived of her inheritance from her father and her paternal grandfather of the Earldom of Lennox – which went to King James – and her paternal grandmother's jewellery; so on her father's death she became entirely dependent on her maternal grandmother. Fortunately Bess was one of the wealthiest women in England through her four marriages, and it was obvious that Arbella and her mother would not starve, a fact well known both to James and Elizabeth, which may be one reason for their later behaviour towards her. Elizabeth apparently did have some pangs of conscience over the treatment of the young girl and drew up plans to allow Arbella's mother £400 and Arbella £200 a year out of the sequestered Lennox estates.[5]

Negotiations over this allowance were still going on when Arbella's young mother Elizabeth died suddenly on 21 January 1582. She was a warm-hearted and much-loved woman, and the death of her favourite child was a terrible blow to Bess. Her stepfather, the Earl of Shrewsbury, wrote a letter on the day of her death to Lord Burghley and the Earl of Leicester:

> My very good Lords, – It hath pleased God to call to his mercy, out of this transitory world, my daughter Lennox, this present Sunday, being the 21st of January, about three of the clock in the morning. Both towards God and the world she made a most godly and good end, and was in most perfect memory all the time in her sickness even to this last hour. Sundry times did she make her most earnest and humble prayer to the Almighty for her Majesty's most happy estate, and the long and prosperous continuance thereof, and as one most infinitely bound to her Highness, humbly and lowly to beseech her Majesty to have pity on her poor orphan Arbella Stuart, and, as at all times, heretofore, both the mother and poor daughter were most infinitely bound to her Highness, so her assured trust was that her Majesty would continue the same accustomed goodness and bounty to the child she left; and of this her suit and humble petition, my said daughter Lennox, by her last will and Testament requireth both your lordships (to who she found and acknowledged herself most bound), in her name, most lowly to make this humble petition to her Majesty . . .
>
> My wife taketh my daughter Lennox's death so grievously that she neither doth nor can think of anything but of lamenting and weeping.
>
> I thought it my part to signify to both your lordships in what sort God hath called her to his mercy, which I beseech you make known to her Majesty, and thus with my very hearty commendations to both your lordships I cease.

To the Right Honourable my very good lords, my Lord Burghley, and
my very good Lord and cousin the Earl of Leicester, of her Majesty's
Most Honourable Privy Council.[6]

A second letter, written in a similar vein, was sent on the same day to
Sir Francis Walsingham.

As we have seen, after the death of his father, Lord Darnley, James
considered himself heir to the Earldom of Lennox on the death of his
grandfather Matthew Stuart. By a similar token, when his uncle Charles
Stuart died, he felt that the Earldom should revert back to him for him
to dispose of as he wished, there being no male heir. He proceeded to
grant the Earldom to Charles's elderly uncle, the Earl of Caithness. He
resigned it in 1581 to James in favour of his favourite Esmé Stuart, Lord
d'Aubigny. To salve his conscience over his cavalier treatment of his
cousin Arbella, he suggested, much to Queen Elizabeth's alarm, that
Arbella marry Esmé Stuart. However, the Queen's hostility to the idea
prevented him from proceeding any further.[7]

Bess, shattered by the early death of her child, was sufficiently recovered after a week to write to Sir Francis Walsingham, the Secretary of
State, and to Lord Burghley, the Lord High Treasurer, to make sure that
the £200 allowance from the Queen to her granddaughter would still be
paid. Arbella's grandmother was determined that she should be brought
up and educated as a future Queen of England under her guidance. In a
pleading letter to Sir Francis Walsingham she points out that the cost of
Arbella's education is very expensive and suggests that the £400-a-year
allowance which had been granted to her mother and which lapsed at
her death should be used for this purpose. She wrote:

Good Mr Secretary, – With my right hearty commendations, I pray you
take it in good part my like desire that it will please you to prefer my humble suit unto the Queen's Majesty in the behalf of a poor infant, my jewel
Arbella, who is to depend wholly upon her Majesty's bounty and goodness, being in her tender age deprived of her parents, whose late mother
in her extreme sickness, and even at the approach of her end (which I
cannot without great grief remember), did most earnestly sundry times
recommend to her Majesty's gracious goodness and favour that poor
infant her only care, with hearty desire and confidence that her Majesty
might enjoy a long and prosperous reign, and be a gracious patron and

sovereign to that her innocent child, as her Majesty hath hitherto been to them both, and for as much as the four hundred pounds yearly granted to my lady daughter is by her death at the Queen's disposition, my humble suit is that her Highness, whose manifold gracious favours and bounty have so much bound me as no subject can be more to a most worthy sovereign, will vouchsafe to grant the same four hundred pounds to Arbella for her maintenance during her minority, which is but for a few years, whereof I doubt not that her Majesty will favourable accept as hitherto she has done of all my suits, and consider that her bringing up every way as appertaineth and so as she may the sooner in service to attend upon her Majesty (which I chiefly desire) will hardly be performed with six hundred pounds yearly in money, the more commodity is not to be made of the lands, being as they are in lease. I do not like that she should be now here as she was with her mother in her lifetime, neither can I be contented she be in any place where I may not some time see her and daily hear of her well-doing, and therefore at great changes to keep her in house with such as are fit to attend upon her and be in her company, and being near well to being seven years old, she is of very great towardness to learn anything, and I very careful of her good education, as if she were my own and only child, and a great deal more for the cosanguinity she is of to her Majesty, whose happy reign over us I daily with the most zealous mind pray the Almighty Governor of all things long to continue . . . Sheffield, this 6th May. Your loving friend E. Shrewsbury.[8]

A similar letter was sent to Lord Burghley. She received no answer to either. As Bess was known to be one of the wealthiest women in England it would have occurred to most that she could afford to pay for the education of her granddaughter herself. Besides, her allusion to Arbella's close relationship to the Queen, implying that she was a possible heir to the throne, was sufficient to turn Elizabeth against the child. Raising the issue of succession to the Queen was like waving a red rag at a bull, so this was a major tactical blunder on Bess's part.

Arbella was six and a half years old when her mother died and was a clever and good-looking child. Sir Walter Mildmay, who used to visit Mary Queen of Scots at regular intervals, may have met her at Chatsworth as early as 1577 or seen her at her Lennox grandmother's home in Hackney. He wrote of Arbella in 1588, when she was thirteen years old, a year before his death, that she was pretty and resembled her paternal grandmother.

Having received no answer to her letters to Walsingham and Burgh-ley, Bess wrote once more to them on the subject of an education allowance for her granddaughter, again rather ingenuously mentioning her close blood link to the Queen, but she got no reply and received only the £200 for the child's allowance. In the event, no expense was spared in the education of the little girl and as well as being an excellent scholar she also became an accomplished horsewoman and very good dancer.

Up to 1577 the Earl and Countess of Shrewsbury were on extremely good terms, his letters to her showing that he still adored her. But shadows were gathering around the marriage. The Earl was finding the job of custodian to Mary Queen of Scots irksome and extremely expensive. Bess did not like toing and froing between her husband's many houses as the Scottish Queen was moved about – the household was obliged to move with her – and she longed to spend more time at her beloved Chatsworth. She was also growing increasingly jealous of her husband's obvious devotion to the Queen of Scots. In a letter to him written from Chatsworth in 1577, while he was staying with the Queen of Scots and Arbella at Sheffield, she wrote, 'I have sent you lettuce for that you love them, and every second day some is sent to your charge and you let me know how you, your charge and love doeth and commend me I pray.' The wording of this letter is opaque, but it was from this time that the relationship between them deteriorated rapidly.

Gilbert Talbot, the Earl's second son, was devoted to Bess – his mother-in-law and stepmother – taking her side in all arguments and reporting in detail on the Earl to Bess in his letters to her. As she spent more and more time at Chatsworth, the Earl became very angry with her, and Gilbert reported his father as saying, 'What, is she gone from Sheffield? Is her malice such that she will not tarry one night for my coming? You know, Gilbert, how often I have cursed the building at Chatsworth for want of her company. You see she careth not for my company, by her going away. I would not have done so to her for £500.'

It would appear that Gilbert aggravated the bad feeling between the couple by his remarks, and the relationship was only temporarily patched up by their mutual sorrow when the old Countess of Lennox died in 1578.

Bess, in spite of her failure to get more than £200 out of Queen Elizabeth for Arbella's maintenance, still called her granddaughter Countess of Lennox as did Mary Queen of Scots, and the title appears on an anonymous English painting of her aged thirteen. Moreover Arbella seems to have retained a little estate called Smallwood in Cheshire which belonged to her grandmother, Margaret Lennox. A record still exists of a court case over rents due to her from it, but the income would have been negligible.

In 1583 Francis Talbot, the eldest son of the Earl of Shrewsbury, died, making Gilbert heir. Grave disputes as to property and inheritance arose from this death, and the deterioration in the relationship between Bess and her husband accelerated from this time. Strangely, some of Bess's children sided with the Earl and some of his with Bess. It was William and Charles Cavendish who stood firmly by their mother during the increasingly acrimonious quarrels, and Henry, her eldest son, who was married to Grace Talbot, sided with his stepfather, whereas Gilbert, his son, stood on the side of Bess.

Queen Mary was allowed a household of thirty individuals when she was first committed to the care of Shrewsbury, but owing to his laxity the number grew to forty-one. Shrewsbury never got an adequate allowance for her upkeep, and it was estimated that he was about £10,000 a year out of pocket over her expenses. Shrewsbury was well aware that in the absence of any direct heirs to Elizabeth – and the young age of King James and Arbella – on Elizabeth's death it was possible that Mary might come to the English throne. He was therefore fairly indulgent towards her with respect to her desire for company and for engaging in open-air pursuits such as hunting. She visited some of the great families of the area, such as the Manners and Pagets, and was also, after many requests to the Queen, allowed to take the waters at nearby Buxton to alleviate muscular problems – now diagnosed as one of many symptoms of porphyria.

The arrival in England in 1580 of two famous Jesuits, Father Edmund Campion and Father Robert Parsons, had a profound effect on the already hard-pressed recusant Catholic population – and on Mary Queen of Scots. However much she tried to keep her religion out of politics – and the Jesuits were also committed to that policy – the Jesuit Mission aggravated the anger of the government against them and made Mary's position as Catholic heir to the throne more problematic.

It is interesting to speculate that in Campion's tours of the north of England he most likely met the captive Queen and Arbella. Gervase

Pierrepoint – a relative of Sir Henry Pierrepoint who married Bess's daughter Frances – was his travelling companion. It is known that he spent the Christmas of 1580 with the Pierrepoint family at Holme Pierrepoint in Nottinghamshire. It is also known that he stayed with Bess's other daughter Mary Talbot at Sheffield, where Mary Queen of Scots spent much of her time in the company of the young Arbella. Maybe Campion reported back to Parsons that Arbella, being brought up a staunch Protestant by her grandmother, was of no interest to them as a rival or successor to Elizabeth.

The symptoms that Mary displayed are so similar to those that overtook Arbella later on that the description of them by Macalpine and Hunter in their paper 'Porphyria in the Royal Houses of Stuart, Hanover and Prussia', published in the *British Medical Journal* on 6 January 1968 , is worth quoting.

Mary Queen of Scots is one of the great invalids of history, not only the great tragic figure. Contemporaries said she suffered from the spleen, the rheum, and fits of the mother. Medical historians have refined these into gastric ulcer, rheumatism and hysteria. From her late teens she suffered attacks of which the essential features were excruciating abdominal pain and vomiting, painful lameness, fits and mental disturbance – a combination suggestive of porphyria. So notorious were her colics that her son who never lived with her knew of them and recognized his own afflictions in hers, as he told his own physician, the great Theodore Mayerne.

The most severe attack, in which she nearly died, occurred at Jedburgh in 1566 when she was 24 years old. Its rapid onset and alarming symptoms followed by quick recovery gave rise to the suspicion still lingering in some quarters that she was poisoned. She had had attacks of sickness and colic for some years, when she was suddenly taken ill, became strange in manner, nauseated and sleepless. The next day she developed a terrible pain in her side, made worse by every movement, even breathing. She vomited continuously, it was said, more than sixty times, eventually bought up some corrupt blood. She became delirious, two days later lost her sight and speech, had a series of fits, remained unconscious for some hours and was thought to be dead. Yet within ten days she was up and about again. In 1570 the same symptoms recurred . . . Attacks often confined her to her bed and she was melancholy, excitable or distracted. This mental instability, together with her recurrent invalidism and inability to move her limbs, her grievous pain in her side, and her equally inexplicable recoveries, impressed those around her as histrionic and she was believed to use illness as occasion demanded to gain her ends. Mary Queen of Scots shares with many sufferers from porphyria, living and dead, the fate of being judged hysterical.[9]

Her niece Arbella was to suffer the same fate.

The house at Chatsworth was a very fine mansion. There was a great flowering of domestic architecture in the Elizabethan age, and the remarkable work of Bess of Hardwick in designing and building the great houses at Chatsworth and Hardwick Old and New Halls exemplifies this well. The house that Sir William Cavendish bought at Chatsworth was largely in ruins, and Bess transformed it into a magnificent residence fit for a Queen – and for her little granddaughter whom she looked on as heir to the throne.

The cost of rebuilding Chatsworth amounted to around £80,000. It faced east and had four turrets and was built around a quadrangle. The rooms were panelled in oak and hung with wonderful tapestries, while much of the furnishings, silver and plate was transferred from the Cavendish house in London. Queen Mary's bower still exists in the garden near the bridge, overlooking the river. It is a tranquil raised walled garden reached by a long flight of steps and surrounded by a moat. The steep steps up to it lead to a barred gate which opens on to a small garden overlooking the river. Even when taking the air Mary would have been closely watched in this garden retreat, with guards mounted on the steps behind her, the moat and the locked door as extra security. It is the only part of the garden at Chatsworth that today appears neglected. Mary paid several visits to Chatsworth between 1569 and 1584, the comfort of Bess's house making a welcome contrast to the dreary conditions she had endured at Tetbury Castle, Staffordshire. Chatsworth remained the same as Bess left it on her death until 1686, when her great-great-grandson, the fourth Earl and first Duke of Devonshire, began making major alterations to the south front. He obviously inherited his craze for rebuilding from Bess, because he was so delighted with the work he had carried out that he then tackled the east front, the formal gardens and the cascade. He subsequently turned his attentions to the west and north aspects during the years 1669 to 1702, the house being completed in 1707 just before he died.

It was in 1583, when Arbella was seven years old, that Bess bought Hardwick Hall, her old home, which was by then in a dilapidated state, for £9,500 and started to rebuild it as a future home for her second son, William, Chatsworth already being destined for the eldest son, Henry.

Arbella was surrounded by a great retinue of servants who treated her like royalty; her apartments were sumptuous and every attention was paid to the quality of her education. Great importance had been placed on the education of high-born females from Henry VIII's time, influenced by the example of the household of Sir Thomas More, and Arbella had excellent tutoring in the classics, philosophy and languages, in all of which subjects she excelled, and her love of literature was to be a comfort to her all her life. However, being indulged excessively by her grandmother, her uncles and aunts and servants was very damaging to the child, who became overbearing and spoilt. This may have been one of the reasons why her grandmother turned against her, as her hopes of attaining the throne for Arbella dwindled.

But in 1583 Arbella's star was still in the ascendant, and Elizabeth's favourite, the Earl of Leicester, saw a chance of a highly advantageous marriage for his infant son, the Baron Denbigh, who was then only two years old. This scheme, hatched by Leicester and Bess, went as far as the two children becoming engaged and exchanging portraits. Mary wrote to Mauvissière, the French Ambassador, about it in 1583, begging him to inform the Queen of how much she disapproved of the match for her little niece. When Elizabeth heard of it she was very angry with Leicester, and he was out of favour for some time, until the untimely death of his son aged three.

The next matrimonial plan came in 1584 from Elizabeth herself, who suggested that Arbella should marry James Stuart. In fact it would have been an excellent solution to the problem of the succession, but James, who was eighteen at the time, had no desire to marry, although he was angry with Leicester for trying to marry his son to Arbella. Four years later James married the Danish Princess Anne. It was also in 1584 that Philip II of Spain first suggested that Arbella should marry one of the sons of the Duke of Parma, descendants of John of Gaunt. The matter arose again in 1590.

In July that year a serious dispute broke out between the Earl of Shrewsbury and William and Charles Cavendish over land he had given to Bess when they married. This did nothing to improve Bess's already problematic relationship with her husband, leading to furious quarrels, and Arbella found herself in a very stressful atmosphere. The onerous responsibility that the Earl had as custodian of Mary Queen of Scots had turned him into a worried, petulant man, who saw his fortune being eroded not only by the expense of maintaining the Scottish Queen but also by the extravagant tastes of his wife.

For taking the part of the Earl in the ensuing arguments, Bess's eldest son Henry was immediately evicted from Chatsworth, the best of the furnishings being sent to Hardwick Old Hall. As the Earl's daughter was married to Henry, the Earl decided to seize the house back from William and Charles Cavendish who had taken possession of it. On July 1584 he rode to Chatsworth from Sheffield with forty horsemen and demanded to be admitted, declaring that the house and the goods that had been taken from it were his property. As the Earl had bequeathed all this property to Bess on their marriage, the Cavendishes refused to give it up, and the enraged Earl then went to the Queen and begged for a legal separation from his wife. The Queen would not hear of it and suggested that Bess should live at Hardwick with an income fixed by the Lord Chancellor and Leicester. Bess was against the idea, as she was still prepared to tolerate living with her husband. In fact, they did try to live together again, but the Earl's implacable hatred of her from this point on made it impossible.

That year, in an attempt to protect her granddaughter from the family squabbles, Bess sent Arbella to stay with her various relatives, sometimes with the Cavendishes and sometimes with the Talbots. Charles Cavendish remarked, 'How she profiteth in her books, and I believe she will dance with exceeding grace and can behave herself in great proportion to every one in their degree.'[10] Arbella also spent time in London with her tutors and staff at the town house of the Earl, partly to keep her within the notice of the Queen.

Shrewsbury was weary of his long custody of Mary Queen of Scots, and in 1585 he persuaded the Queen to relieve him of his post. Sir Ralph Sadler was given the job for a short time and handed her over to Sir Amyas Paulet, who had been Governor of Jersey, later that year. Paulet was a stern man, and all Mary's hopes of escape were dashed when he removed her to the hated Tetbury Castle. Throwing caution to the wind, she started a secret correspondence with Anthony Babington, and, with the connivance of Sir Francis Walsingham, she continued to write to him until she was totally implicated in Babington's plot to kill Queen Elizabeth and place her on the throne instead. She was subsequently taken to Fotheringhay Castle in Northamptonshire the following year to stand trial for treason and was condemned to death by execution.

The Earl of Shrewsbury was appointed Chief Commissioner for her trial and execution. By that time he was a deeply unhappy old man, permanently estranged from his wife and some of his children. From his stepson Henry came the disturbing report that, rather than take the blame for the public execution of her cousin, the Queen had asked Sir Amyas Paulet to strangle her. He was deeply shocked at the idea and refused to carry out her wishes.[11]

On 8 February 1587 Mary was duly executed. Gilbert Talbot was present and watched his father give the sign to the executioner to kill her. The old Earl wept as her head fell. Sir Walter Mildmay, who had so admired Arbella when she was a little girl, was present as a commissioner and had refused to allow the executioner to stay in his house, Apthorpe, which was near Fotheringhay.

Gilbert was ordered to leave Fotheringhay at one o'clock the next morning and ride to London to tell the Queen that Mary was dead. The execution of her aunt was a great blow to Arbella. So much of her early childhood had been spent in Mary's company that her brutal death filled Arbella with fear and horror. Moreover, she was well aware of how precarious her own position was.

With the death of Mary, Arbella's political significance was not lost on Queen Elizabeth. James was naturally very angry about his mother's death, and the Queen lost no time in using the little girl as a pawn in her game with him. Soon after Mary's execution in 1587 she summoned Arbella to court to dine with her. Bess was delighted but decided that Arbella should be presented to the Queen by Mary Talbot and Charles Cavendish and not herself, as she was still out of favour over her broken marriage.

It was the first time that the Queen had set eyes on the young girl who was a contender for the throne. Arbella behaved beautifully, and the Queen was very taken with her. She always dined in an inner chamber with a few attendants, and Arbella had the great honour of joining her there. After the meal the Queen introduced her to various nobles and ambassadors who had dined in the outer apartment. Among them was the wife of the French Ambassador, Madame d'Aubespine de

Châteauneuf, who was very impressed to hear Arabella speak excellent French. 'Look well at her,' said the Queen, 'for she is not so unimportant as you may think. One day she will be even as I am and will be Lady Mistress, but I shall have been before her.' The Ambassador himself was also very taken with the young girl and described her as 'having much understanding, speaking Latin, French and Italian well, sufficiently handsome in the face, and without doubt would be the lawful inheritor of the Crown if James of Scotland was excluded as a foreigner'.

Arbella possessed many qualities that Elizabeth would have wished to find in an heir; she was Protestant, born in England, young enough to train and with a good mind. It was short-sighted of her not to recognize this. Elizabeth loved using people as pawns in her game of keeping people guessing as to her successor, at great cost to those members of her family who were involved, and she continued to play this game until she was dying and unable to speak.

Lord Burghley had been a great friend of the Shrewsbury family for many years, and he was particularly attentive to Arbella on this visit to court. After she left the Queen he invited her to supper at his house where she met, among others, Sir Walter Raleigh, on whom she made a very good impression. Burghley asked her to come again, and Arbella maintained her friendship with him. In July 1588, after a visit to London with her aunt and uncle, the Talbots took her to say goodbye to the old man, but he was unable to see them, so they wrote to him a letter of thanks to which Arbella added a postscript in French. 'Je prieray Dieu Monsr, vous donner en parfaice et entière, santé tout heureux, et bon succès et sècrez tousjours preste à vous faire tout honneur et service. Arbella Steward.' This is the earliest known example of her handwriting.[12]

BESS'S TROUBLESOME CHARGE

In 1588, the year of the threatened Armada invasion from Spain, Arbella left court with the Talbots, owing to spoilt and arrogant behaviour on her part which upset the Queen and her courtiers. She went to the great mansion of Wingfield, a magnificent house eleven miles south of Chesterfield, another property of the Earl of Shrewsbury, which had been admired even by the highly critical Queen of Scots who had spent some of the happiest days of her captivity there. This second visit to court, which took place in the spring of 1588, had not been a success. It was noted that Arbella was much more confident this time and had upset many of the court ladies by trying to take precedence over them. Her behaviour, which suggested that she regarded herself as the Queen's heir, displeased Elizabeth, and Arbella fell out of favour.

In November 1588 her tutor and steward Nicholas Kynnersley wrote a worried letter about Arbella to Bess at Chatsworth. 'My Lady Arbella at eight of the clock was merry and eats her meat well, but she went not to school these six days, therefore I would be glad of your ladyship's coming, if there were no other reason.'[1] Bess, who was already growing alarmed at the unpredictable behaviour of her 'jewel Arbella', no doubt hurried to Wingfield to chastise the wayward girl. Arbella's refusal to attend to her studies was certainly out of character.

Despite the Queen's displeasure with her cousin at court, she was still enquiring after her to the old Earl in 1589. But she did give up her attempts to obtain Arbella's estates for her in Scotland. Arbella had inherited the small estate of Smallwood in Cheshire. Bess also gave up trying to get her Lennox estates from the Crown. She did, however, have the girl's portrait painted this year by an unknown artist, aged thirteen and dressed in white satin and pearls; it is inscribed 'Arbella Stuarta, Comtissa Leonine [Countess Lennox], aetasi, 13 Anno Domini 1589'. Although she never received the jewels her paternal grandmother left her, the pearls she is wearing in this painting may have been part of her inheritance from Mary Queen of Scots or her mother.

Although the Earl of Shrewsbury was very fond of Arbella, before his death in 1590 he began to have grave doubts about her moodiness and bouts of odd behaviour. Sir John Harrington, godson of Queen Elizabeth and a well-known wit and author, however, described her in glowing terms when he met her at Wingfield, aged thirteen. 'She was reading French out of Italian, Italian and English out of both', much better than he could, and he praised her 'virtuous disposition, her choice education, her rare skill in languages, her good judgemental sight of music, and a mind free of pride, vanity and affectation, and the greatest sobriety in her fashion of apparel and behaviour. I myself have been an eye witness, having seen her several times at Hardwick and at Chelsea, where she made me read the tale of Drusilla in Orlando to her, and censured it with a gravity beyond her years.'[2]

The Earl unburdened himself to a trusted servant, saying that he feared that Arbella would 'bring much trouble on his house by his wife and her daughter's devices, that she was wont to have the upper hand of his wife and her daughter Talbot, but now it is otherwise (as it has been told me) for that they have been advised by some of their friends at court that it was misliked'.[3]

There is no doubt that from around this time Bess's attitude towards her granddaughter changed for the worse and she treated her more harshly and more like a prisoner. This made Arbella, already wayward, more inclined to behave badly; it also perhaps accelerated the onset of the disease that was later to overwhelm her. However, Bess must still have had some affection for the girl, as in a will made at this time she left Arbella £1,000 and much valuable jewellery.

It was not only Arbella's behaviour at court that caused her to be out of favour. The vitally important question of whom she should marry as well as the many plots that were centred on her – particularly after Mary's execution – were also a cause of the Queen's growing displeasure. Knowing what we do of Elizabeth's antagonism to matrimony among her courtiers and near relations, it is doubtful that she ever had any intention of allowing Arbella to marry. Elizabeth used the prospect of marriage merely as a weapon to get what she wanted.

But for Arbella to contemplate marriage without the Queen's permission was unthinkable. However, in 1586, when she was ten, English

Catholics were already hatching plots to kidnap her, intending to convert her to Catholicism and marry her off to a foreign prince. In 1590 a candidate materialized in the person of Rainutio, the eldest son of Alexander Farnese, Duke of Parma. As he married elsewhere while negotiations were still in progress they switched their attentions to his second son, Cardinal Farnese. The Pope agreed to give him dispensation from his vows, and he had a small claim to the English throne through his descent from John of Gaunt's eldest legitimate daughter, who had married John I of Portugal. •

Sir William Stanley, an adventurer and a brilliant former servant of Elizabeth in Ireland, was the principal agent of the plot. He was a staunch Catholic, by now unhappy in his service to the Queen and in the pay of the Spanish government. He talked openly in Flanders, where he was then living, of his plans to capture Arbella and take her first to Flanders and thence to Spain. Stanley's involvement in the plot was revealed in the confessions of two priests, Father Young and Father Thomas Christopher, probably under torture. There is no evidence that Arbella herself was involved in the plotting, and even her staunchly Catholic aunt Mary Talbot, although suspected of having some knowledge of the conspiracy, was never charged with complicity.

Arbella suffered by being used as a tool not only by Elizabeth but by James, who decided to extend friendly overtures towards her at the end of 1591. His first letter to her – the only one to survive – runs as follows:

The King of Scotland to Lady Arbella Stuart. Although the natural bonds of blood, my dear cousin, be sufficient for the good entertainments of amity, yet will I not abstain from those common offices of letters, having now for so long kept silence till the fame and reports of so good parts in you have interpelled me. And as I cannot but in heart rejoice, so can I not forbear to signify to you hereby, what contentment I have received hearing of your so virtuous behaviour, wherein I pray you most heartily to continue, not that I doubt thereof, being certified of so full concourse of nature and nourriture, but that you may be the more encouraged to proceed in your virtuous demeanour, reaping the fruit of so honest estimation, the increase of your honour and joy, and your kindly affected friends, specially of me, whom it pleaseth most to see so virtuous and honourable scions arise out of that race whereof we both have our descent. Now hearing more certain notice of the place of your abode, I will the more frequently visit you by my letters, which I would be glad to do in person, expecting also to know from time to time of your estate by your own hand, which I look you will not weary to do, being first summoned by me, knowing how far I shall be pleased thereby. In the meanwhile, the next occasion of further knowledge of your state, after my heartiest commendation, I wish you, my dear cousin, of God all honour and hearty contentment.

From Holyrood House, the 23rd of December 1591.[4]

From now until the end of Elizabeth's reign there were to be no more dinner parties with the Queen for Arbella, or honours paid to her by ambassadors. A stern letter was written to Bess by Burghley in September 1592 warning her of plots involving her granddaughter and commanding her to keep a close watch on her. Bess's reply makes it chillingly clear how already, at the age of sixteen, Arbella was being closely guarded by her grandmother night and day for fear of her making an imprudent marriage or being kidnapped by supporters of foreign powers, particularly Spain, to force her into a Catholic union.

My Honourable Lord – I received your lordship's letter on Wednesday towards night, being the 20th of this September, by a servant of Mr John Talbot's of Ireland. My good lord, I was at the first much troubled to think that so wicked and mischievous practices should be devised to entrap my poor Arbell and me, but I put my trust in the Almighty, and will use such diligent care as I doubt not but to prevent whatsoever shall be attempted by any wicked persons against the poor child. I am most bound to her Majesty that it pleased her to appoint your lordship to give me knowledge of this wicked practice, and I humbly thank your Lordship for advertising it; if any such like be hereafter discovered, I beseech your Lordship that I be forewarned. I will not have any unknown or suspected person to come to my house. Upon the least suspicion that may happen here, any way, I shall give advertisement of it to your Lordship. I have little resort to me; my house is furnished with sufficient company. Arbell walks not late; at such time as she shall take the air, it shall be near the house and well attended on; she goeth not to anybody's house at all; I see her almost every hour in the day; she lieth in my bedchamber. If I can be more precise than I have been I will be. I am bound in nature to be careful of Arbell; I find her loving and dutiful to me, nor more by me regarded

than to accomplish her Majestie's pleasure, and that which I think may be
for her service. I would rather wish many deaths, than to see this, or any
such like wicked attempt to prevail. About a year since there was one
Harrison, a seminary, that lay at his brother's house about a mile from
Hardwick, whom I thought then to have caused to be apprehended and
to have sent him up, but found he had licence for a time. Notwithstanding, the seminary soon after went from his brother's house, finding how
much discontent I was with his lying so near to me. Since my coming now
into the country, I had some intelligence that the same seminary was
come again to his brother's house, my son William Cavendish went
thither of a sudden to make search for him, but could not find him. I write
thus much to your Lordship, that if any such traitorous and naughty persons (through her Majestie's clemency) be suffered to go abroad, that
they may not harbour near my houses, Wingfield, Hardwick nor
Chatsworth in Derbyshire; they are the likest instruments to put a bad
matter in execution.

One Morley, who had attended on Arbell and read to her for the
space of three years and a half, showed to be much discontented since my
return to the country in saying he had lived in hope to have some annuity
granted him by Arbell out of her land during his life, or some lease of
ground to the value of forty pound a year, alleging that he was so much
damnified by leaving the University, and now saw that if she were willing,
yet not of ability, to make him any such assurance. I, understanding by
divers that Morley was so much discontented, and withal of late having
some cause to be doubtful of his forwardness in religion (though I cannot
charge him with Papistry), took occasion to part with him. After he was
gone from my house, and all his stuff carried from him, the next day he
returned again, very importunate to serve without standing up on any
recompense, which made me more suspicious, and the more willing to
part with him. I have another in my house who will supply Morley's place
very well for the time. I will have those that shall be sufficient in learning,
honest and well disposed, so near as I can. I am enforced to use the hand
of my son William Cavendish, not being able to write so much myself, for
fear of bringing great pain to my head. He only is privy to your Lordship's
letter, and neither Arbell, nor any other living, nor shall be.

I beseech your Lordship, I may be directed from you as occasion shall
fall out. To the uttermost of my understanding, I have been and will be
careful. I beseech the Almighty to send your Lordship a long and happy

life, and so I will commit your Lordship to his protection. – From my house at Hardwick the 21st September, 1592.[5]

Thomas Morley, known as the 'singing man', had a reputation for being an amateur spy of Cecil's and a fine musician. He graduated from Oxford in 1588 and in 1591 became organist at St Paul's Cathedral. In 1592 he became a Gentleman of the Chapel Royal. It is highly likely that he spent the gap of three and a half years after leaving university as tutor to Arbella in Bess of Hardwick's household at Hardwick Hall.[6]

In 1594, Father Parsons, a Jesuit who had been sent to England with Father Edmund Campion, wrote a pamphlet under the name of Richard Dolman setting out the positions of the various claimants to the English throne, including that of Arbella. Elizabeth was furious. Although the Jesuits were well aware of Arbella's proximity to the throne, they had not up to this point supported her claim on the grounds that she was not a Catholic and that she was descended from the second marriage of her paternal grandmother and therefore might be illegitimate. The Catholic party was under the impression that Lord Burghley would be a strong supporter of Arbella's claim after Elizabeth's death, and it was even suggested that he had plans to marry her to his son.

He again suggested, in 1592, that she should marry Esmé Stuart. Such a marriage would have pleased James in several ways. For a start he would have assuaged his guilty conscience about depriving Arbella of her Lennox estates. He had also made Esmé Stuart his heir in the absence of any children of his own, which would have joined their claims to both the Scottish and English thrones, and it would have enhanced the prestige of his favourite. Elizabeth was completely against the marriage and poured scorn on James for suggesting it. From an outsider's point of view, it would seem to have been rather a good plan, but even Arbella's maternal relatives did not support it. The problem of the lack of an heir for James was resolved with the birth of Prince Henry in 1594.

More marriage plans for the unfortunate Arbella were disclosed by the Duke of Sessa in a letter to the King of Spain. He claimed that the Pope suspected that Queen Elizabeth was trying to persuade Henry IV of France to put away his wife and marry Arbella, who would then become her heir. Rumours of this plot by Elizabeth made James desperate, and he contacted the King of Spain, promising that he would become a Roman Catholic if the King would support his claim to the

English throne. He foolishly mentioned that one of his complaints against the Queen was the Act of Parliament that had been passed just before his mother's execution, stating that no person who was descended from anyone who had conspired against the Queen should inherit the throne. Legally, under that Act, James was barred from the succession.

Henry IV was a dispassionate observer of all these goings-on. The diplomat the Duc de Sully wrote in his *Mémoires* that, on the possibility of Henry's marriage to Marguerite of Valois being dissolved, the King would have no objection to an alliance with the Infanta of Spain, provided that he would gain power over the Low Countries; neither would he refuse the Princess Arbella of England if 'since it is publicly said that the crown of England really belongs to her, she were only declared presumptive heiress of it. But there is no reason to expect that either of these things will happen.'[7] The fact that Arbella herself was indifferent to the Crown makes it all the more tragic that her life was to be dominated and finally destroyed by those who were either fanatical that she should inherit it or prepared to go to any lengths to prevent her from doing so.

Until 1601 Arbella still spent time with Mary and Gilbert Talbot, who had accompanied her to court. She seemed to be increasingly out of favour with the Queen, but in 1600 New Year gifts were exchanged between her and her aunt and the Queen. Lady Dorothy Stafford, a long-serving and devoted lady-in-waiting to Elizabeth, wrote on the Her Majesty's behalf a thank-you letter to the Countess, saying that the Queen had been very taken with a beautiful scarf sent to her by Arbella. The Countess must have been writing to the Queen on Arbella's behalf, for Lady Dorothy stated that she would do her best to help her. 'It pleased her Majesty to tell me,' she wrote,

> that whereas in certain former letters of your ladyship's, your desire was that her Majesty would have that respect of my Lady Arbella that she might be carefully bestowed to her Majesty's good liking; that according to the contents of those letters, her Majesty told me that she would be careful of her, and withal hath returned a token to my Lady Arbella, which is not so good as I would wish it, nor so good as her ladyship deserveth in respect of the rareness of that which she sent unto her Majesty. But I beseech you, good madam, seeing it pleased her Majesty

to say so much unto me touching her care of my Lady Arbella, that your ladyship will vouchsafe me so much favour as to keep it to yourself, not making any other acquainted with it but rather repose the trust in me for to take my opportunity for the putting her Majesty in mind thereof, which I will do as carefully as I can.[8]

Obviously the situation was one of the utmost delicacy, to be handled with kid gloves.

To understand Arbella's final fall from grace and banishment from the royal court we have to consider her friendship with Elizabeth's handsome young favourite the Earl of Essex. There is little doubt that Arbella had fallen in love with him and that some sort of relationship existed between them . There was quite a lot of gossip about them at the time, some of which must have reached the Queen's ears. But it is only in Arbella's letters after his death that light is shed on their clandestine meetings. In a letter of 1603, written on Ash Wednesday, the second anniversary of his death, she pours out her grief for his loss and refers to the increasing slights that she has received from the Queen.

Arbella's wayward behaviour during this period has never been satisfactorily explained but perhaps makes more sense if her affection for Essex is considered as the first great love of her life. Her love and loss of him, exacerbated by the onset of porphyria – with its symptoms not only of great physical pain and illness but severe mental inbalance and disturbance – may help to explain the numerous letters about her relationship with him that reached the Queen after Essex's death and Arbella's subsequent banishment from court and imprisonment at Hardwick.

It was at this time that she became estranged from the Talbots, and as they were very close to Sir Walter Raleigh, a sworn enemy of Essex, their disapproval of Arbella's relationship with Essex, which seems to have so angered the Queen and perhaps ruined Arbella's chances of inheriting the Crown after her death, can well be understood. In 1602 Lord Henry Howard wrote of the high ambitions that the Countess of Shrewsbury, a close friend of Raleigh's, had for her niece. 'The league is very strong between Sir Walter Raleigh and the Lady Shrewsbury and Sir Walter's wife, Elizabeth Throgmorton. She [Elizabeth] is a most dangerous woman and full of her father's inventions.' Sir John Harrington, in his *Tract on the Succession to the Crown* written in 1601–2, wrote, 'My Lady Arbella came to be spoken of, and much commended, as she is well worthy of many noble parts, and the Earl of Essex in some glancing speeches gave occasion to have both himself and her honourable friends to be suspected of that which I suppose was no part of their meaning.'

Arbella would have been very attractive to the hugely ambitious Essex, and the relationship between them was a very dangerous affair indeed, to be hushed up as far as possible by those who wished Arbella to succeed the Queen. It must certainly have contributed to Essex's downfall and to that of Arbella.

PRISONER AT HARDWICK

Hardwick Hall, standing high over the Derbyshire countryside, is an awesome sight and is today considered one of the great masterpieces of Tudor architecture. This monument to Bess of Hardwick's genius for building is more of a palace than a private house, and she no doubt had in her mind that it might one day be used as such by the future Queen Arbella. However, Hardwick Hall – 'more glass than wall' – is not what it first appears to be: a light, airy, pleasant building. It has an atmosphere of mystery and gloom, as if the tragic spirit of the young woman who was imprisoned here by her grandmother, threatened by madness, still wanders through the High Great Chamber and the Long Gallery.

This was never a great home like Chatsworth but, rather, built to impress, the rooms getting larger, the windows higher and no doubt the house colder as you went from the ground floor to the top. Arbella mentions the cold, the great length of the Long Gallery, where she was able to have a private conversation at one end out of earshot of her grandmother at the other end, and of standing round the fire of the Lower Great Chamber trying to get warm. On grand occasions Bess and her granddaughter would dine in state in the High Great Chamber; the food must have always been cold as the kitchen was a great distance away. Meanwhile the Low Great Chamber would have been used on less formal occasions for meals. The family rooms on the first floor comprised a fairly comfortable drawing-room, Bess's chamber, Arbella's chamber and the chamber of Bess's favourite son, William Cavendish. Arbella is likely to have spent a great deal of time reading in her room but had to sleep in the same chamber as her grandmother, another factor that must have been detrimental to their relationship.

In 1601 Bess made an inventory of the contents of Hardwick House. The furnishings of Arbella's room were opulent and comfortable.

In my ladie Arbell's chamber: six peeces of hangings of yellowe, blewe and other coloured damask and sattin wrought with golde flowers and trees and lined with canvas, a bedsted, a mattris, a downe bed, a wooll quilt, a bolster, a pillow, a payre of fusteans [cotton blankets], three spanish blankettes, a white fledge [eiderdown], a Canapie of Chaungeable taffetie laced and fringed with white and red silk, three Curtains of the same stuffe to it, a Cubberd, a Carpet for it of nedleworke wrought with antickes and frettes, with green silk frenge and lined with watchet sarcenet, a square table, a Carpet for it of russet velvet paned with gold and silver and layed with golde and silver lace and Frenge about lyned with yelloe and grene sattin bridges, a long narrow quition [cushion] of silk needleworke wrought with leaves and knotes with red silk fringe and lined with black sattin bridges, and another long quition wrought with knotes with yellowe, red and grene silke frenge and lyned with black Damask, ten peeces of Darnick [a type of fabric manufactured in Tournay], a Joyned stoole, a fier shovell, a payre of tonges, waynscott under the windows.[1]

The inventory for Bess's bedroom has the entry, 'My Lady Arbell's bedsted, a canopie of darnix blewe and white with gilt knobs and blewe and white frenge, a Cloth of checker work of cruell about the bed a mattriss, a fether-bed, a bolster. A quilt, four spanish blanketes, a coverlett.' This bed sounds a more humble affair than the one in her own chamber. Two four-posters in Bess's room, even though it is quite a good size, would have been a squeeze.

After the death of Essex in February 1601 Arbella returned to Hardwick in the autumn of that year to nurse her grief, never to return to Elizabeth's court. Closely guarded by her grandmother, who was unable to share her grief, and ostracized by her favourite aunt and uncle, it was at this time that the symptoms of physical and mental illness began to manifest themselves. Her letters of this period, some coherent and some reading like the ravings of a lunatic, confirm that she is unwell.

Mary Queen of Scots was twenty-four when she went down with what has now been diagnosed as a severe bout of porphyria. Arbella was nearly twenty-seven when similar symptoms developed. Her chaplain, John Starkey, writes of her longing to escape from Hardwick and his anxiety about her bouts of uncontrollable grief. She looked upon him as a trusted friend, and it is not surprising that the rumour spread that he was in love with her. 'She thought of all the means by which she could leave home, by reason she was hardly used,' he said, 'in spiteful and dis-graceful ways . . . after as time being at her books she would break forth into tears.'[2]

Bess had threatened to take away her jewellery, the sale of which could have helped her to escape, and it was Starkey who helped her have it removed to Yorkshire. He was a discontented, unhappy man who had acted as tutor to William Cavendish's son for nothing except his keep, and he decided to leave Hardwick and promised to help Arbella escape if he could. They exchanged gifts, which added to the scandal, but in the end he proved a broken reed: being unable to sort out his own affairs he committed suicide. Arbella borrowed money from him and still owed him about £80 at his death. Any involvement with her was dangerous, and it may have been as a result of threats from the Queen that he killed himself, a frightened as well as a disillusioned man.

In July 1602 the Jesuit Father Anthony Rivers wrote, 'I hear some have the intention to marry the Earl of Hertford's second son with Arbella, to carry it [the succession] that way, but these "supra nos nihil ad nos"'(they are over us but they are nothing to us).'[3] The rumours connecting Arbella with the Hertford family gathered momentum. First, it was his eldest son, Lord Beauchamp, who had recently been widowed, that she was apparently to marry. Next, Lord Beauchamp's eldest son, Edward, aged sixteen, was the favourite and later his second son, William, then a boy of fourteen. Such a huge difference in their ages would not have been a bar if the marriage had been a suitable one. But Arbella could not have fixed on a more unsuitable match for herself, one guaranteed to arouse the full wrath of the Queen.

Over forty years earlier the Earl of Hertford had become betrothed to Lady Jane Grey's younger sister Catherine, and in the early days of Elizabeth's reign they were secretly married. The Earl's mother, the Duchess of Somerset, knew nothing of this, and to try to control her wayward son she suggested to the Queen that he should be sent to Paris. Not daring to disobey a royal order, he went, but shortly after his depar-ture it became obvious to the court that Lady Catherine Grey was preg-nant, and news of the marriage soon reached the Queen's ears. She immediately imprisoned Catherine in the Tower. A marriage between two people who, through their close relationships to Jane Seymour and Lady Jane Grey, were so close to the throne was unthinkable. The Earl was recalled immediately from France and placed in isolation in the

Tower. They were examined separately on 12 September 1561, and each gave identical accounts of their clandestine marriage. Nine days later, on 21 September, Catherine gave birth to a son, Lord Beauchamp. The Queen pronounced him illegitimate and, as the couple never asked the name of the Lutheran priest who officiated at their wedding and the only other witness, Jane Seymour, had since died, they found it difficult to prove that they were legally married. Most of their friends believed them, however, and the warders of the Tower allowed them to meet. The outcome was a second son, Lord Thomas Seymour, who was born on 10 February 1563.

The Queen's fury increased, and she put the illegitimacy case to the Court of the Star Chamber, and the Earl of Hertford was fined the enormous sum of £15,000. An outbreak of plague, however, forced Elizabeth to allow the young couple to be moved from their prison. Catherine went to stay with her uncle, Sir John Grey, and the Earl went to his mother's house in Tottenham. They were both closely guarded and never saw each other again. Finally, after five years of imprisonment and separation from her husband, Catherine's health deteriorated and she was removed to Cockfield Hall, the private house of Sir Owen Hopton, Governor of the Tower, where she died on 28 January 1568. The Earl continued to live as a house prisoner for another nine years. On his release he was a broken man and, although he married again twice, he spent his life trying to prove the legitimacy of his two eldest sons. He is buried beside Catherine in Salisbury Cathedral. Moreover, although the Earl was eventually granted his freedom, Queen Elizabeth never forgave him for marrying Catherine, and he lived in terror of her for the rest of his life.

Thus, Arbella must have been fully aware that the Earl and the Queen would be horrified at the idea of his grandson marrying a woman as near to the throne as herself without the Queen's consent and that he would feel he was repeating his original crime in the Queen's eyes. But partly through Arbella's desperation to get away from her grandmother and partly through lack of judgement – perhaps affected by illness – she was not deterred. Bess strongly disapproved and would have nothing to do with it, but Henry and William Cavendish, secretly thinking it would be a brilliant match for Arbella, remained neutral.

There was a rumour that Hertford had sent his lawyer, Kirton – whose son had married Bess's stepdaughter (a daughter of Sir William

Cavendish by a previous marriage) – to Wales to see Owen Tydder, whose son was Arbella's page, about a possible marriage between her and Hertford's grandson. Arbella was determined to get in touch with the Earl and persuaded John Dodderidge, an elderly retainer at Hardwick, against his will, to take a message from her directly to the Earl. He had much to lose, as Bess was responsible for his son's education and he leased a farm on the estate. He left on Christmas Day 1602, Henry Cavendish lending him a horse, no doubt to annoy his mother. Arbella made notes for the message which Dodderidge was to give the Earl. She suggested that the boy and an older man travel up to see her in disguise.

If they come to me themselves they will be shut out at the gates; if locked up, my grandmother will be the first to complain to the Queen. If dismissed they must fully prove themselves to be no sycophants of me. For the first let them make some offer to sell land, and Mr Hancock and Mr Proctor are good patterns to follow, so that they shall have whom they will to tarry in the house, and be welcome for a longer time than shall need. I desire this may be some ancient grave man; the younger may come as his son or nephew, and tarry or go away as we shall then think good. For the second, I protest your witness, either by word or writing, shall fully satisfy me. But it will be counted discretion in you, and confirm their good opinion of me, if you require them to bring all the testimonies they can, as some picture or handwriting of the Lady Jane Grey, whose hand I know, and she sent her sister a book at her death, which were the very best they could bring, or of the Lady Katherine, or Queen Jane Seymour, or any of that family that we know they, and none other but they, have. And let some of the company be of my Uncle Henry's acquaintance, who yet must not come to the house because of my Aunt Grace and his servants, but shall meet him at some other place. Their care is no more but to come speedily and secretly to Mansfield, or some place near and after you, and such intelligence as you have in the house will provide for the rest.[4]

The rest of the note is quite incoherent.

The luckless Dodderidge arrived at Tottenham on Monday 30 December while the old Earl was at dinner. Dodderidge rather tactlessly insisted on speaking to him at once, even though other people were present, whereupon he fell on his knees and poured out the story of the proposed marriage. The Earl was appalled and insisted that he put the matter in writing so that he could place it before the Privy Council. Dodderidge was locked in a room overnight. Frightened, he hastily wrote a letter to Arbella – which she never received – informing her of his plight, and the following morning he was taken to Sir Robert Cecil, who immediately informed the Queen. She was filled with rage to think that the hated Hertford should be involved with Arbella, and, on Cecil's advice, on 1 January sent Sir Henry Brounker, a Queen's Commissioner, to Hardwick to investigate the matter. He arrived there on 3 January 1603.

Sir Henry was a man of great tact who had been well chosen by Cecil to handle two difficult women. When he arrived, Bess, William Cavendish and Arbella were walking in the Long Gallery. Giving the Queen's compliments to Bess, he handed her a letter which made it clear that he had come to speak to her granddaughter. He conducted Arbella to the other end of the gallery – well out of earshot of her grandmother and uncle – and after a few niceties accused her of plotting to marry Hertford's grandson. She flatly denied the charge but, after further questioning, admitted that she had asked Dodderidge about the matter. Sir Henry then produced her instructions to Dodderidge, and her terror so increased that she became quite incoherent. He suggested that she retire to her room and write down everything that she knew about the matter.

The document she produced was a rambling jumble of words that he was quite unable to comprehend, and he asked her to try again. Her second effort was as bad as the first. Unable to get any sense out of her, Sir Henry decided to leave Hardwick on 10 January and return to London. He was involved in a bad fall from his horse on the journey back and finally arrived at Lambeth on 13 January. By then the elderly Queen was too ill to see him – she had started to decline in February 1602 after the death of the Countess of Nottingham – so he wrote down an account of his visit to Hardwick. Meanwhile he asked Sir Richard Bulkeley to examine the old retainer Owen Tydder, but he got no useful information from him.

Bess wrote to the Queen on 9 January, just before Sir Henry left Hardwick, begging her to place Arbella in another house, have her wait on her at court or find a suitable husband for her. Arbella, still in great distress, wrote to her aunt, Mary Talbot, begging her to come to Hardwick to see her, but she got no reply to her letter, a sign that the Talbots were still angry with her over the Essex affair.[5] Bess wrote again to the Queen complaining of Arbella's wild talk of having a secret lover. Meanwhile Cecil and Vice-Chamberlain Sir John Stanhope wrote to Bess on the Queen's behalf suggesting that the harsh restrictions on her granddaughter should be lifted.

> Some base companions, in the Queen's opinion, have taken advantage of Arbella's youth and sex to deceive her with the idea that Hertford wishes her to marry one of his grandsons, which from the incongruity of ages is, on the face of it, untrue. Vexed as her Majesty is with the concealment of the matter, she is willing to pass over the offence this time, on the condition that she takes this mishap for a warning, and confides any other project to her grandmother or the Queen. Lady Shrewsbury is not to exclude people or to guard her house any longer (which causes gossip), but everything is to return to its accustomed routine; a trustworthy gentlewoman is to keep her eye on Arbella's doings, but otherwise no extraordinary restraint is to be used, and she may ride and walk about as usual. The Queen, however, will not hear of relieving the countess of her troublesome charge.[6]

When Arbella read their missive she was very relieved, and she wrote a sensible, undated letter to the Queen thanking her for her clemency. But it was obvious that the situation between Bess and Arbella was unchanged, for she then penned an incoherent, rambling piece of prose to her grandmother hinting at an unknown lover whose name would only be revealed to the Queen. Her mental state was aggravated by the tragic news that Starkey had committed suicide on 2 February.

On 2 February she wrote to the Queen again complaining that she was still as closely guarded and constrained by her grandmother as ever and asking for Sir Henry Brounker to return.[7]

THE MYSTERY OF ARBELLA'S BEHAVIOUR

Arbella seems to have been mentally unstable at this time, although she had short periods of sanity and lucidity. On 16 February 1603 she wrote a good letter to her cousin, Edward Talbot.

> Feb. 16th, 1603. Noble Gentleman . . . I request you most earnestly to deliver a message from me to her most sacred Majesty, which shall be greatly to her Majesty's contentment, your honour's behalf, and is of great importance. It requireth great haste, and I have advertised a most honourable Privy Councillor that I have sent for you to employ you in her Majesty's service, so that you may not excuse yourself or lose time in your own respect, whom it concerns more ways than this. And of your own honourable disposition I doubt not that you would bestow a journey hither, and so to the court for my sake. Your father's love, and your grateful friend Arbella Stuart . . .

> P.S. I pray you in kindest manner commend me to my Lady Ogle, and sweet Mrs Talbot whom I am very desirous to see; and entreat her to hasten you hither, for the sooner you leave the better for us all.[1]

In spite of the tender messages to his wife and sister-in-law, Edward did not come to Hardwick. Although he took Arbella's side against her grandmother, he evidently had no desire to get involved in what was becoming a very nasty affair. Five days later the Countess wrote to Cecil not only of her grave worries over the state of her granddaughter but in despair at the situation for herself.

> February 21st, 1603. Sir – I must beseech you to bear with my often troubling you. Since my late letter to you, Arbell hath been very sick with extreme pain in her side, which she never had before, so as I was in great fear for her . . . She hath had a doctor of physic with her for a fortnight

together, and enforced her to take much physic at this unseasonable time, but finds little ease. I see her mind is the cause of it all. She saith that if she might speak with Sir Henry Brounker or some other sent from her Majesty, she should be well; for that she hath a great desire to satisfy her Majesty in all matters, whose gracious favour and good opinion she desireth above all earthly things. Good Mr Secretary, my most earnest suit is that it will please you to be a means to her sacred Majesty, for the speeding sending down of Sir Henry Brounker, or some other, to whom Arbell is desirous to declare sundry things which she saith she will utter to none but one sent from her Majesty. The Almighty ever prosper her Majesty with continuance of his great blessing. And so desiring good Mr Secretary to hold me excused for importuning you in this sort, I will take my leave, praying God to grant you all honour and happiness. From Hardwick, this 21st February 1603. Your most assured loving friend E. Shrewsbury.

P.S. Arbell is so wilfully bent that she hath made a vow not to eat or drink in this house or where I am, till she may hear from her Majesty, so that for preservation of her life I am enforced to suffer her to go to a house of mine called Oldcoats, two miles from here. I am weary of my life, and therefore humbly beseech her Majesty to have compassion on me, and I earnestly pray you to send Sir Henry Brounker hither.[2]

Although the Queen was gravely ill, she was aware from the communications received from Arbella and her grandmother that Arbella, whom many looked on as her rightful heir, was mentally unstable. The timing was unfortunate, and under normal circumstances Arbella would have been able to contain her feelings and restrain herself. But if her derangement was the result of porphyria – triggered off by her stressful circumstances at Hardwick – she would have been incapable of controlling her behaviour.

Cecil reacted promptly to Bess's letter and sent Sir Henry back to Hardwick with a letter for Bess. Arbella was to be brought back from Oldcoats by 2 March to be questioned by Sir Henry again. She was obviously still very ill; her replies to the many questions put to her about her secret lover were all the same.

'Who was it against whose love she had so long stopped her ears, though he never requested anything, but was more for her good and

honour than his own?' The reply came back, 'The King of Scots.' 'Who
had been so worthily favoured by her Majesty, and had done her so
much wrong?' 'The King of Scots.' And so the interrogation went on
through the lengthy interview, the same answer given to each question.
In despair Sir Henry sent her to her room and told her to write down
what she felt, after getting her to sign his document with her nonsensical
answers. Sir Henry returned to London the next day.

Immediately Sir Henry had departed Bess wrote to Cecil and Stanhope. It was obvious that the tough old lady had come to the end of the
road with her difficult granddaughter, finally realizing that she was out
of her mind. She wrote:

> May it please you, Sir Henry Brounker will make relation of all that hath
> passed here, which may ease you of reading, and keep me from writing of
> a long discourse, of that which to my infinite grief I find. It is not
> unknown to you what earnest and important suit my unfortunate Arbell
> hath made for Sir Henry Brounkner's coming down. I was in hopes
> she would have discovered somewhat worth his travel, but now she will
> neither name the party to whom she hath shown to be so affectionate, nor
> declare to Sir Henry Brounker any matter of moment, spending the time
> in idle and impertinate discourse. And though Sir Henry Brounker hath
> left nothing undone that might bring her to conformity, he could not in
> any sort prevail with her, though she put him in hope from time to time
> that she would name the party.
>
> If it had lain well in my power to make all things plain as I had a desire
> to further Sir Henry Brounker's service, it had been less trouble to him
> and he should not have departed with such uncertainties. This is the first
> fruit of them that have laboured to draw her natural affection from
> me, and to persuade her to all these vanities. They little respected her
> undoing so they might overthrow me with grief. Soon after Sir Henry
> Brounker's departure hence, I look she would fall into some such extrem-
> ity [that is, refusing to eat or drink or to see Bess] as she did lately. She
> said before Sir Henry Brounker that if she had not been suffered then to
> move hence, she would have performed her vow, and the like I daily
> doubt she may do upon any toy she will take discontentment at.

Bess states quite clearly that the rift in her family, particularly her
strong dislike of her eldest son, Henry Cavendish, had exacerbated the

situation between her and Arbella. Bess continues:

> And therefore I most earnestly beseech you both to be a means to her
> Majesty for her speedy remove; it may be the change of place will work
> some alteration in her. Sir Henry Brounker can testify how careful I am
> to keep her quiet till I may understand further of her Majesty's pleasure.
> She most vainly had prefixed a day to Sir Henry Brounker for her
> remove. Both he and myself advised her not to stand on days or times.
> She is so wilfully bent and there is so little reason in most of her doings,
> that I cannot tell what to make of it. A few more weeks as I have suffered
> of late will make an end of me. Notwithstanding if it might be for her
> Majesty's service, I could be content to spend my life; but I have had over
> great trial, now that she is bought to this extremity, that her remaining
> here is like to breed over-great inconveniences which will not lie in my
> power to prevent.[3]

The letter Arbella wrote to Sir Henry Brounker on 2 March on his
departure was relatively lucid. She starts:

> I take Almighty God to witness, I am free from promise, contract, mar-
> riage or intention to marry, and so mean to be whilst I live, and nothing
> whatsoever shall make me alter my long determination, but the continu-
> ance of these disgraces and miseries, and the peril of the King of Scots his
> life, and if her Majesty continue her hard opinion of me, and I continue in
> my lady my grandmother's hands, then whatsoever befall, I have deter-
> mined of a course which, if it please her Majesty to like of, will be for her
> Majesty's honour and best to my liking.

She implies further on in the letter that she only pretended to have a
lover to persuade the Queen to send an emissary such as Sir Henry to
Hardwick to resolve her intolerable position *vis-à-vis* her grandmother.
She finishes: 'I will make a vow if it shall please her Highness to command, upon condition that I may reobtain her Majesty's favour, and
have my dear and due liberty, I will never marry whilst I live, nor entertain thought, nor conceal any such other matter whatsoever from her
Majesty, which I shall think worthy for her Majesty to incline her
princely ear unto.'[4]

This letter, one of the four in Arbella's own hand kept with the Cecil

Papers, is smudged with tears. Her next to Sir Henry, written on the following day, is mainly incomprehensible, her derangement apparently triggered by the incidents described in the more lucid parts of the letter. She had evidently been followed through the great rooms of Hardwick Hall by her grandmother hurling abuse at her and, like the old woman, she was in despair at the failure of Sir Henry's visit.

This letter, written on 4 March, is a remarkable mixture of insanity, humour, erudition and vivid description.

> Sir Henry, – I cannot but wonder at your light belief when great ones tell you incredible tales, and incredulity when you have heard the word and oath of a Puritan for a certain truth. If your commission be not to examine such great ones as I presume to accuse in matters of truth, alas what a dwarf I am thought at Court. If your commission stretch not beyond the Albian Cliffs and Cheviot Hills, I would I were with that most noble gentleman, who I constantly affirm (but will not swear) to be the King of Scots, and then we should agree in our tales, and make true English, whereas now I think even you are doubtful of what will become of us. Truly I can tell, and I will tell you truly, even as I told you, even as I would have it. For if I do not, or rather have not since I saw you, broken some of your good friends of their will, I am greatly deceived. For whereas if the noble gentleman you would needs suspect had been transported by some Archimedes to Newstead miraculously, especially to himself, as certain Romans (these Romans were full of unsuspicious magnanimity) were hoisted over the walls of the besieged Syracuse, and drawn by one poor scholar (who lightly are not the wisest or strongest faction) through the town; which feat I think, unless you will believe for the author, my disgraced friend Plutarch's sake, you are like never to see executed by an architect, mathematician or engineer living – I will not swear, but I tell you as I think.

After several more bizarre sentences she launches into a description of the goings-on at Hardwick after Sir Henry left for London. 'After my cousin Mary and I had spent a little breath in evaporating certain court smoke, which converted into sighs, made some eyes beside ours run a-water, we walked in the great chamber, for fear of wearing out the mats in the gallery (reserved for you courtiers), as sullenly as if our hearts had been too great to give one another a good word, and so to dinner.' She obviously felt she knew Sir Henry well enough to tease him, and her sense of humour remains despite her distress and anger.

'After dinner,' she continues:

> I went in reverent sort to crave my lady my grandmother's blessing. Which done, her ladyship proved me a true profit, and you either a deceived or deceiving courtier; for after I had with the armour of patience, borne of a volley of most bitter and injurious words, at last wounded to the heart with false epithets, and an unlooked for word, only defending myself with a negative (which was all the words I said, but not that I could have said in my defence) I made a retreat to my chamber, which I hoped by your charter should have been a sanctuary you came with authority you said, and I saw it under two hands, Cecil's and Stanhope's signatures, that might have made any but me believe your word should have gone as current as the word of a prince, or the Great Seal of England – by which I might have recovered a little land which a most noble great-great-uncle of mine [Henry VIII] gave his niece [Margaret Douglas] when he bestowed her on a noble exiled gentleman, but I knew by what was past what would be, and provided thereafter.[5]

Her walk with Mary Talbot after Sir Henry's departure seems to have taken place in the Long Gallery, and the dinner that followed, as the grand guest had departed, would have been taken in the Lower Great Chamber, Bess probably partaking of her meal in the little dining chamber next to it. Having asked for her grandmother's blessing, she was met by a tirade of wrath. Arbella returned to her room which was on the same floor, through the drawing-room, the screams of abuse from her grandmother raining down on her as she and Bess's son William followed her. Of the privacy promised by Cecil and Stanhope there was no sign, much to Arbella's anger, and as she sat down and wrote her first letter to Sir Henry they stood watching over her and then proceeded to read it. She complains of the continued pain in her head and her side, which had laid her up for some weeks. But she must have been getting better, for having finished the letter she went in search of a messenger and eventually found some of the household gathered round the fire in the Upper Great Chamber. It was here that she discovered George Chaworth, who was wearing her glove in his hat. He was married to Bess's half-niece, Mary Kniverton. A lawyer, he was a friend of Arbella's and acted as a carrier of her letters to Sir Henry.

She wrote another short note to Sir Henry on 4 March, also quite rational, which was taken to London by Chaworth.

Sir Henry, – This gentleman, Mr Chaworth, can witness my many great and increased wrongs which, if you will not believe, I cannot help; if you do, and help not to redress to your power, I think you do not discharge the charge imposed on you by her Majesty to see my treatment according to my condition and desert, nor the trust I have reposed in your sincerity and fair promises. Unregarded menaces I assure you shall neither daunt me, nor the worst that any mortal creature can do unto another shall not exhort a thought out of my mouth. Fairer means might have laden you home with that treasure you came for without a quittance; but now I have no more to say to you, but I will say no more, think, say or do what you list. Hardwick this Friday, Arbella Stuart.

P.S. I deal better with you than you with me for I do not torture you with expectation, nor promise better than I will perform.[6]

There is a imperious tone as she firmly puts Sir Henry in his place. Arbella wrote to Sir Henry nearly every day from the time he departed on 3 March – the day after his arrival – until Ash Wednesday, 9 March, when she wrote an enormously long and rambling missive. Madness is evident in many of its pages, perhaps triggered by the fact that Ash Wednesday was the second anniversary of the death of Elizabeth's favourite, the Earl of Essex. Now for the first time she reveals her own devotion to Essex. 'Doth her Majesty favour Lady Katherine's husband [the Earl of Hertford] more than the Earl of Essex's friend? Are the Stanhopes and Cecils able to hinder or diminish the good reputation of a Stuart?' She then turns to the hated henchman of the Cecils, Mr Holford, who was acting as a spy for him, carrying messages to and from Hardwick. Back again to the Earl of Essex: 'How dare others visit me in my distress when the Earl of Essex, then in high favour, durst scarcely steal a salutation in the privy chamber, where howsoever it pleased her Majesty I should be disgraced in the presence in Greenwich, and discouraged in the lobby at Whitehall, it pleased her Majesty to give me leave to gaze on her, by trial pronounce me to be an eaglet of her own kind, worthy even yet to carry her thunderbolt and prostrate myself at her feet (the Earl of Essex's fatal, ill-sought, unobtained desire).'

Arbella then refers to the chaplain, Mr Starkey, for whom she also grieves. She implies that he did not commit suicide because he did not get the living he wished for but because of his connection with her. 'You saw what despair the greatness of mine enemies and the hard measure I have received (and my fortune is not yet bettered), drove innocent, discreet, learned and godly Mr Starkey into; will you be guilty of his blood?' But Essex dominates the letter, and she now gives us a first-hand account of his fatal last encounter with the Queen.

He could go neither friend nor foe knew whither, till he arrived amongst his unwitting enemies from whom he ever returned with honour, and was received home with joy. Till all ungrateful not to be bound more strictly by a letter of her Majesty's hand than all the bonds and commandments of any or all other mortal creatures – he stole from his charge as if he longed for the most gracious welcome he received, and was punished for his unmannerly (but I think in a lover's opinion pardonable) presumption of kissing that breast in his offensively wet riding clothes, with making those mild kind words of reprehension the last that ever his ear received out of his dear mistress's mouth. Of whose favour (not in respect she was his sovereign, as I protest he ever said to me) how greedy he was even in the Earl of Leicester's time (before he so fully possessed it by many degrees, as after, to her Majesty's eternal honour he did) I, and I doubt not many more better believed at court, are good witnesses. And how over-violently hasty (after two years' silent meditation) to recover it he was this fatal day, Ash Wednesday and the new dropping tears of some, might make you remember, if it were possible you could forget. *Quis talia fando temperet a lacrimis? Myrmidomina Dolopumue aut duri miles Ulisses?* And were I unthankfully forgetful if I should not remember my noble friend, who graced me, by her Majesty's commandment disgraced orphan, unfound ward, unproved prisoner, undeserved exile, in his greatest and happiest fortunes, to the adventure of eclipsing part of her Majesty's favours from him, which were so dear, so welcome to him? Shall not I, I, say, now I have lost all I can lose or almost care to lose, now I am constrained to renew these melancholy thoughts by the smarting feeling of my great loss; who may well say I never had nor ever shall have the like friend, nor the like time to this to need a friend in court.[7]

The Queen never recovered from the death of Essex and mourned him bitterly. Arbella shared her grief. There can be little doubt after reading her letter that one of the main reasons for her falling from grace at court was her friendship with Essex. She mentions a little later that James had listened to the court scandal about her relationship with him. The mortal illness of the Queen was kept a secret from most people, and it is obvious from her writing to the Queen – and expecting a reply – that Arbella did not know that she was so ill. But the news was filtering through, and the Jesuit Henry Garnet wrote the day after Ash Wednesday that the Queen was very sick and that Arbella was likely to be sent up shortly to be guarded. But although Elizabeth was near death she was aware of Arbella's bizarre behaviour and was deeply angry about it.

Arbella's hysterical behaviour before the first more obvious signs of illness developed in her have generally been ascribed to her growing animosity towards her grandmother and her mounting frustration and anger at being confined at Hardwick. Her incoherent letters have generally been ascribed to hysteria and 'madness'. The few biographers of her life have always said that her behaviour at this time remains a mystery.

Both Mary Queen of Scots and Arbella tended to hysteria, both were considered mentally unstable and both had the accompanying symptoms of acute pain in the side, acute headaches and muscular weakness. Arbella had complained of trouble with her eyes, another characteristic of porphyria. With James I we have meticulous medical notes kept by his physician Sir Theodore Turquet de Mayerne, and James often mentioned that he suffered from the same symptoms as his mother. These included intermittent bouts of acute pain, vomiting, mental instability and discoloured, purplish urine, as well as periods of uncontrollable weeping. His illness may well account for his erratic treatment of Arbella when he became King, sometimes treating her with great kindness and generosity and at other times with callous cruelty.

Major research has been conducted into the hereditary disease of porphyria in the House of Stuart by Dr Ida Macalpine, Dr Richard Hunter and Dr C. Rimmington in 1968 and in the excellent book *Purple Secret* written by Professors John Röhl, Martin Warner and David Hunt in 1998. It now seems that Arbella's physical and mental breakdown was an early manifestation of variegate porphyria. There is strong evidence that Mary Queen of Scots inherited the illness from her father, James V.

Porphyria is more common in women, especially those of child-bearing age. It is more likely to remain latent in men, who none the less pass it on to the next generation. Charles I showed no symptoms of the illness but certainly passed it to one of his children. Five times in the history of the royal family what has now been recognized as porphyria was treated as suspected poisoning: the nearly fatal illness of Mary Queen of Scots at Jedburgh in 1556; the death of James's son Henry, Prince of Wales, in 1612; James I's death in 1625; and that of Charles I's youngest daughter, Henrietta, Duchess of Orléans, in 1670 and of her daughter, Marie Louise, Queen of Spain, in 1689.

George III's strange and tragic illness more than a century later was diagnosed as porphyria during the 1960s. But from whom did he inherit it? It was discovered through the detailed medical notes of Dr Theodore Mayerne that James I, his great-great-great-grandfather, had suffered from the disease and he had inherited it from his mother Mary Queen of Scots. It was also revealed that Prince Henry and Henrietta of Orléans died from the condition as well. But who was the common ancestor of James I and Arbella who could have passed on this illness to them both? They were first cousins, with a common antecedent in Margaret Tudor, elder daughter of Henry VII.

Examining George III's descendants, there is good evidence that nearly all his children suffered from symptoms of porphyria. Queen Victoria's medical history makes her a suspect. Charles Greville wrote on 12 December 1858, 'The Queen is so excitable that the Prince Consort lives in perpetual terror of bringing on the hereditary malady.' She certainly passed on the fatal gene to her daughter Vicky, who in turn passed it to her elder daughter, Charlotte, whose daughter Feodora (1879–1945) also had the disease. Alexandra, the Tsarina of Russia, who was directly descended from Mary Queen of Scots, also appears to have had it. In our present day Prince William of Gloucester was diagnosed with the illness but died in a plane crash. The medical records of Princess Margaret may well lead to the conclusion that she, too, was a sufferer.[8]

With its wide range of symptoms, porphyria can be difficult to diagnose, but the presence of a combination of them enables one to recognize its presence. One of the remarkable features of the illness is how quickly the patient can recover, particularly from the bouts of madness. It was so with Arbella, who seemed to recover quickly from her mental instability and was plotting her escape from Hardwick soon afterwards.

6

THE KING'S DEAR COUSIN

Arbella was still far from well, and while she was writing almost daily between 3 and 9 March 1603 to Sir Henry Brounker she was also planning her escape from Hardwick with the help of her uncle Henry Cavendish and a Catholic friend, Henry Stapleton. The two men were staying at an inn at Mansfield, a village about two miles from Hardwick, with up to forty servants placed at strategic points round the nearby countryside. On Ash Wednesday Arbella sent her servant Henry Dove and her page Richard Owen to Henry to tell him that she planned to escape from Hardwick the following day to Hucknell, a little village about half a mile from Hardwick. She was expected to arrive on foot, and Henry and Stapleton went to the house of a Mr Facton to wait for her, while a servant of Facton's, John Stark, waited out of sight of Hardwick with horses in case she needed one. Anxiously waiting for her, they decided to ask the vicar, Mr Christopher Chapman, if they could have the key to the church which possessed a steeple with a commanding view of Hardwick. While they were waiting for the key Owen and Arbella's embroiderer Freake arrived with a message from Arbella to say that her grandmother – who had evidently discovered the plot meanwhile – had refused to allow her to leave the house.

Henry became very angry and went to the gates of Hardwick and demanded to see Arbella. Bess, who had quarrelled with Stapleton some years before, refused to allow him in, but she could not forbid her son to enter, and she was well aware, much as she disliked him, that he was playing a very dangerous game in trying to help his niece to escape, as this could be regarded as treason. On entering the yard Henry took Arbella by the hand and led her to the gate, but Bess refused to allow it to be unlocked. A furious scene took place, which drew a large crowd on both sides of the gate, with Arbella screaming that she was being held a prisoner. Finally Henry was forced to return to Mansfield and Arbella was forbidden by her grandmother from leaving the house again.

The episode finally brought Bess to the end of her tether with her granddaughter, and she wrote to Cecil demanding that she be removed from Hardwick at once. As soon as Cecil heard of Arbella's attempted escape he sent Sir Henry Brounker back to Hardwick, where he arrived in record time on 17 March. It was obvious that he had not come merely to check on her condition but to interrogate the people involved in the plot. Stapleton escaped to London, but Henry, Christopher Chapman, Henry Dove, John and Matthew Stark, servants to Mr Facton, and Facton himself were all questioned. Henry himself was ordered to go before the Council, but his part in the affair was hushed up owing to the delicate situation resulting from the imminent death of the Queen, still with no heir to the throne named.[1] She had gone downhill since the death of her cousin the Countess of Nottingham, and in the second week of January she had caught a bad cold, which seems to have developed complications by February. By 15 March the Queen was very ill, refusing food and also refusing to go to bed.

From Arbella's point of view, the escape attempt was not entirely unsuccessful, as it was decided to remove her from Hardwick to Wrest House in Bedfordshire, the home of her beloved cousin Elizabeth Talbot, who was married to Sir John Grey, the fifth Earl of Kent. The move could not have come at a better time for Arbella. Parted from her grandmother and living with people she liked, her health improved dramatically, a quick recovery so typical of porphyria. On 20 March Bess wrote a codicil to her will striking out Arbella and Henry as beneficiaries. A letter written by Brounker from Hardwick on 25 March, asking Cecil if he should detain Arbella without a warrant under the Great Seal, implies that she was at Hardwick when the Queen died on the day before. Arbella travelled to Wrest soon afterwards.

For ten days before her death the shrunken figure of the dying Queen had crouched on cushions on the floor of her bedroom at Richmond Palace, refusing to lie in bed, silent, with a finger in her mouth as if she were trying to remember something important she should do. She had still not named an heir. The Council had decided among themselves that James should succeed her, and it would appear that even the Shrewsburys, who were great friends of Cecil, agreed with this. When she was asked if she wanted the King of France to succeed her, she made no answer. Then the King of Scotland was suggested. Still no reply. When they suggested Lord Beauchamp, the son of the Earl of Hertford, she finally spoke. 'I will have no rascal's son in my seat.' Arbella was not mentioned, but Elizabeth's struggling brain would almost certainly have recalled the rumour that she was going to marry Beauchamp's son.

The Queen was finally forced into bed and died a few hours later, in her seventieth year, without speaking again. Arbella was her next of kin in England, and she was asked to attend the Queen's funeral as her chief mourner, but she refused. She was largely recovered from her illness and living quietly at Wrest. If she nursed any ambitions to succeed Elizabeth she would surely have accepted this honour. But she never desired the throne and her unwavering refusal to go to the funeral confirms this. She was deeply hurt at the Queen's treatment of her and by not attending the funeral she stated as much. Since access to the Queen during her lifetime was not permitted, she would not, after Elizabeth's death, 'be brought upon the stage for a public spectacle'.[2]

The Queen was buried near her half-sister Mary in Westminster Abbey on 28 April. Because Arbella did not attend the funeral the nearest relative that could be found for the role of chief mourner was Elizabeth's step-aunt by marriage, the Marchioness of Northampton.

The Earl of Shrewsbury, having signed the proclamation of the new King, was anxious to make a good impression on him, not only for his own sake but on behalf of Arbella. He therefore invited James to spend a night on his journey south at his mansion at Worksop, near Sherwood Forest, which had been built by his father. The King started to travel south on 5 April, arriving on the 20th. As he rode through the park he was met by huntsmen, who had organized a splendid chase, one of James's favourite pastimes. Afterwards a sumptuous banquet was laid on, with excellent musicians to entertain him. He so enjoyed his visit that he made thirteen of the Earl's friends knights before he left the next morning. Arbella was not there to meet him, probably owing to poor health.

Before James reached London he wrote a cordial letter about her to the Earl of Kent.

For as much as we are desirous to free our cousin the Lady Arbella Stuart from the unpleasant life which she hath led in the house of her grandmother with whose severity and age, she, being a young lady, could hardly agree, we have thought fit for the present to require you as a nobleman of whose wisdom and fidelity we have heard so good report to be contented for some short space to receive her into your house, and there to use her in that manner which is fit for her calling, having the rather made choice of you than of any other because we are informed that your nephew is matched with her cousin germain in which respect she will like better of that place than of a stranger's until further order be taken.[3]

Arbella must have been pleased that James was so well disposed to her and had been aware of her tribulations with her grandmother.

James arrived at Whitehall in London on 7 May, and on the 11th he wrote again to the Earl of Kent suggesting that Arbella come to Greenwich, accompanied by her aunt the Countess of Shrewsbury – she had inherited the title on the death of her father-in-law – to meet him.

We have been informed by our cousin the Countess of Shrewsbury of the great desire which our cousin the Lady Arbella Stuart hath to come to our presence thereby to have the better occasion to present her love and duty to us. We do very well approve those desires of hers, and for that purpose are well pleased that she do repair to our court at Greenwich in the company of our cousin the Countess of Shrewsbury, her aunt, where we shall be willing to confer with her and make her know how well we wish her in regard to her nearness in blood and how much it doth content us to understand so much of her good carriage of herself as we do by report of her aunt the bearer thereof.[4]

Her first meeting with James was very successful, in spite of James being shy and uncouth. James suggested to Cecil that she should return again to Wrest, but Cecil, knowing her rebellious temperament at being constrained physically, suggested to the King that she should be told that she could choose where to live but that he would make sure that she decided to stay with the Marchioness of Northampton, a Swedish woman who was the third wife of William Parr, Catherine Parr's brother. She lived at Sheen, and from there Arbella started a correspondence with Cecil about her financial affairs. Her small allowance of £200 from Queen Elizabeth had ceased with her death and, apart from the pittance from her property at Smallwood, she had no means of support.

Her letters to Cecil are in startling contrast to the ravings that Sir Henry Brounker had had to contend with in March. They are beautifully written, couched in clear, concise language, and brief:

June 26th, 1603. My good Lord, – I humbly thank your lordship for procuring and hastening the King's liberality towards me. I acknowledge myself greatly bound to your lordship, and have sent this bearer to attend your pleasure, whose important affairs I am constrained to interrupt with this necessary importunity. From Sheen, Arbella Stuart.[5]

James was bombarded with similar requests to attend him at court at the beginning of his reign, and it shows his high regard for Arbella that he dealt with hers so quickly.

After a spectacular progress, Anne of Denmark arrived at Windsor at the end of June. Arbella did not go to meet her on her journey south but stayed at Sheen until she was summoned to Windsor shortly after the royal arrival. She and the new Queen were the same age and, although quite different in temperament and tastes, Anne being a pleasure-loving, frivolous person and Arbella studious and thoughtful, they took an instant liking to one another. The two elder children, Prince Henry and Princess Elizabeth, were delighted with her too. Anne insisted that she stay at court with her and treated her as the first lady. Arbella was overjoyed. Her new-found freedom and the unfamiliar affection she received from them meant a great deal to her.

On 2 July she watched the installation of Prince Henry as a Knight of the Garter in St George's Chapel, Windsor, with the little Princess Elizabeth. Queen Anne had taken a great dislike to the Earl of Mar in Scotland and refused to attend the ceremony. Arbella left Windsor with the Shrewsburys to stay for a short time in the country, before returning to court at Farnham with them. The plague was then raging in London, so the court was constantly moved from place to place. James had a terror of the disease, but the courtiers found the incessant moving very tedious. Arbella moved with the court to Basing in August, and the Shrewsburys left her to go north for her uncle to take up an appointment as Lord Justice of Eyre, north of the river Trent. Their separation resulted in a number of revealing and informative letters from Arbella who described life at the court with wit and penetrating observation.

The Earl, worried about how his niece would fare at court, expected to hear from her every week. He left her in the care of a relative, Sir William Stewart, who looked after her affairs and reported on her progress regularly to her uncle. One of the matters uppermost in her mind was the pension that James had promised her. Reminded of this by the Earl and Cecil, it was at last paid to her in September, consisting of £800 a year, plus an extra £660 as a present and her 'diet'. The latter was the gift of certain dishes from the royal kitchen every day for herself and her servants. In spite of the King's generosity she found herself getting into debt. Being first lady at court was a very expensive business, demanding a great number of costly clothes as well as constant presents for the royal family.

A vivid picture of court life is evoked by Arbella in a witty letter she wrote to her uncle on 15 September 1603. 'I write to tell you', she wrote:

> of the reason of the delay of Taxis's audience [the Spanish Ambassador, whose audience eventually took place on the 24th at Winchester]. It remaineth to tell how jovially he behaveth himself in the interim. He hath bought great store of Spanish gloves, hawks' hoods, leather for jerkins, and moreover a perfumer; these delicacies he bestoweth amongst our ladies and lords, I will not say with a hope to effeminate the one sex, but certainly with a hope to grow gracious with the other, as he already is. The curiosity of our sex drew many ladies and gentlewomen to gaze at him betwixt his landing place and Oxford, his abiding place . . .
>
> At Oxford he took some distaste about his lodging, and would needs lodge at an inn, because he had not all Christ's College [Christ Church], to himself, and was not received into the Town by the vice-chancellor *in pontificalibus* which they never used to do but to the King or Queen or Chancellor to the University as they say; but those scruples were soon digested, and he vouchsafed to lodge in a piece of the college till his repair to the King at Winchester. Count Arenberg [the Austrian Ambassador] was here within these few days and presented to the Queen the archduke and the infanta pictures, most excellently drawn. Yesterday the King and Queen dined at a lodge of Sir Henry Lea's, three miles hence, at Ditchley, and were accompanied by the French Ambassador and a Dutch duke. I will not say we were merry at the Dutchkin [Duke Ulrich of Holstein, brother of Queen Anne, afterward one of Arbella's suitors] lest you complain of me for telling tales out of the Queen's coach; but I could find it in my heart to write unto you some of our yesterday's adventures, but that it groweth late, and by the shortness of your letter, I conjecture that you would not have this honest gentleman overladen with such superfluous relations . . .
>
> The Dutch lady my Lord Wotton spoke of at Basing proved a lady

sent by the Duchess of Holstein to learn the English fashions. She lodgeth at Oxford and hath been here twice, and thinketh every day until she be at home, so well she liketh her entertainment, or loveth her own country; in truth she is civil and therefore cannot but look for the like which she brings out of a ruder country. But if ever there was such a virtue as courtesy at the court, I marvel what has become of it, for I protest I see little or none of it but in the Queen, who, ever since her coming to Newbury, has spoken to the people as she passeth and received their prayers with thanks, and thankful countenance barefaced, to the great contentment of native and foreign people; for I would not have you think the French Ambassador would leave that attractive virtue of our late Queen Elizabeth unremembered or uncommended, when he saw it imitated by our most gracious Queen, lest you should think that we infect even our neighbours with incivility.

But what a theme have rude I gotten unawares! It is your own virtue I commend by the fail of the contrary device, and so thinking on you, my pen accused myself before I was aware. Therefore I will put it to silence for this time, only adding a short but most hearty prayer for your prosperity in all kinds, and so humbly take my leave. From Woodstock, this 15th of September, your lordship's niece, Arbella Stuart.[6]

James loved being at Woodstock, as the hunting was excellent. But the house was extremely dilapidated, not having been occupied since Elizabeth was kept there as a prisoner in May 1553, after her release from the Tower. There was only very limited accommodation for himself, the Queen and a few courtiers. The rest had to sleep in tents in the garden. Cecil complained bitterly of the discomfort that most of the court endured during their stay there. In October the court moved to Foulston in Kent.

By this time Arbella's excellent relationship with the King and Queen, who had become devoted to her, was threatened by two plots hatched against James to entice Arbella away to the continent, marry her to a Catholic prince and place her on the English throne with the help of foreign aid. They were called the Bye Plot and the Main or Spanish Plot. A great deal of the evidence was suppressed at the time, so it is difficult to determine exactly what happened.

The chief protagonists involved in the Bye Plot were two Roman Catholic priests, Father Watson and Father Clarke, while Lord George

Brooke, Lord Grey of Wilton, Lord Cobham, Brooke's elder brother, and Sir Walter Raleigh were those chiefly involved in the Main Plot. Raleigh always swore that he had been framed by Lord Cobham, who had been a great friend but who spoke against him in court while apologizing for his treachery in private. It says much for the great affection that Arbella had inspired in the King that what could have been a fatal situation for her was dealt with without a word said against her.

The trial of the conspirators in the Main Plot began in Winchester on 17 November, and all the court flocked to it as a great entertainment. Arbella sat in the gallery with the Lord Admiral the Earl of Nottingham, and when her name came up he rose to his feet and addressed the court. 'This lady here doth protest upon her salvation that she never dealt in any of these things, and so she willed me to tell the court.' Cecil also addressed the court in her favour. 'Here hath been a touch of the Lady Arbella Stuart, the King's near kinswoman. Let us not scandal the innocent by confusion of speech. She is as innocent of all these things as I or any man here. Only she received a letter from my Lord Cobham to prepare her, which she laughed at and passed it to the King.'[7] The Attorney General also declared Arbella to be innocent of the affair.

Arbella's health began disintegrating again in October as a result of the pressure she was under. On the 27th she wrote to the Earl that her eyes were very bad and made the same comment in a letter to the Countess of Shrewsbury of 6 November. On 28 November, after the trial had ended, she complained of extreme pains in her head.[8] On 8 December she wrote to her uncle and aunt. In her letter to the Countess she mentioned that she had had an extremely severe cold, a condition that seems to trigger the symptoms of porphyria. Her letter to the Earl of the same date, although more lucid than those she wrote to Sir Henry Brounker, reveal that she was becoming mentally unstable once more. The Countess, realizing that she was ill, sent her a pill and some hartshorn. It is in the letter to the Countess on 8 December that she makes an allusion to the trial.

How defective my memory be in other ways, assure yourself I cannot forget even small matters concerning that great party, much less such great ones, as I thank God, I was not acquainted withal. Therefore when any great matter comes in question, rest secure, I beseech you, that I am not interested in it as an actor, howsoever the vanity of wicked men's vain designs have made my name pass through a gross and a subtle lawyer's lips of late [Coke's speech at Sir Walter Raleigh's trial], to the exercise and increase of my patience and not their credit.[9]

Henry Cavendish had been summoned to London, as he was suspected of being involved in one of the plots. In fact he was not called to give any evidence at the trial.

One of Arbella's great admirers at court was Sir William Fowler, the son of Thomas Fowler, who had been executor to her Lennox grandmother. William had always felt guilty about the jewellery that his father had taken to Scotland, and Sir William wrote of Arbella as the eighth wonder of the world. His letters to Shrewsbury were full of praise for her, and he wrote a sonnet for her, pointing out how far above the frivolities of the court she was:

> Whilst organs of vain sense transport the mind,
> Embracing objects both of sight and ear,
> Touch, smell and taste to which frail flesh inclines,
> Prefers such trash to things that are more dear.
> Thou, godly nymph, possessed with heavenly fear
> Divine in soul, devout in life and grave,
> Rapt from thy sense and sex, thy spirits steer
> Toyes to avoid which reason doth bereave.
> O graces rare! what time from shame shall save
> Wherein thou breath's (as in the sea does fish
> In salt not saltish) exempt from the grave
> Of sad remorse, the lot of worldling's wish.
> Ornament both of thyself and sex
> And mirror bright where virtues doth reflect!
> *In salo sine sale.*[10]

Arbella describes some of the tedious children's games the court ladies played for hours every day when the court was at Winchester. She wrote to her uncle on 8 December:

Whilst I was at Winchester there were certain child-plays remembered by the fair ladies, viz. 'I play my lord', 'Give me a course in your park', 'Rise pig and go', 'One penny follow me', etc. And when I came to court they were as highly in request as ever cracking of nuts was. So I was by the Mistress of revels not only compelled to play as I knew not what (for until that day I had never heard of a play called *Fire*), but even persuaded by the princely example I saw to play the child again. This exercise is most used from ten o'clock at night until three in the morning, but that day I made one it began at twilight and ended at supper time. There was an interlude, but not so ridiculous (as ridiculous as it was), as my letter which here I now conclude.[11]

When not playing these games, much of the day was spent hunting. In an undated letter to the Countess, probably written in late December, Arbella complains about this, as she still feels unwell with the acute neuralgia that was causing her much trouble. She insisted on keeping several hours a day reserved for study – especially of languages and the classics – and Dr Nathaniel Johnstone spoke of having seen a Hebrew Bible in an embroidered cover, which she always took to church.

The court spent Christmas that year at Hampton Court. The Shrewsburys were at Sheffield and sent venison to Hampton Court for Arbella. A great subject of discussion between her and her aunt was what New Year gifts to present to the King and Queen, for as usual Arbella was very short of money. In fact she made a purse for James and gave the Queen two pairs of stockings lined with plush and two pairs of lined gloves. She was on good terms with Cecil, and he gave her a pair of bracelets. It is notable that Arbella's letters to her aunt are full of serious matters, whereas those to her uncle are amusing, frivolous, witty and sometimes long and rambling.

The ladies arrived at Hampton Court on 16 December. The Queen organized a masque and, to Arbella's shocked dismay, gave the Lady Suffolk and Lady Walsingham warrants to remove the clothes of the late Queen from the Tower of London for the performance. As Elizabeth had not been dead for a year this was in extremely bad taste.

Up to the end of January Arbella was still experiencing the eye problems she had had for months, which she mentioned again in a letter to her aunt on 21 January. It is obvious that she was involved with her grandmother's affairs, although no letters between them survive. Arbella's powerful position at court made her a useful mediator in the perpetual family rows that dogged Bess and her children and stepchildren, who were constantly falling out with one another and calling on her for help. The Shrewsburys had not been on speaking terms with Henry Cavendish and his wife since his attempt to help Arbella escape from Hardwick. They decided to make their peace with him by asking him for Christmas and wrote in consternation to Arbella when they received no reply. In a letter to the Earl, written on 3 February 1604, she speaks of arranging a reconciliation between Bess and her eldest son, Henry, and his wife.

I have found so good hope of my grandmother's good inclination to a good and reasonable reconciliation betwixt herself and her divided family, that I could not forbear to impart to your lordship with all speed. Therefore I beseech you to put on such a Christian and honourable mind as best becometh you to bear a lady so near to you and yours as my grandmother is. And think you cannot devise to do me a greater honour and contentment as to let me be the only mediator, moderator and peacemaker between you and her. You know I have cause only to be partial on your side, so many kindnesses and favours have I received from you, and so many unkindnesses and disgraces have I received from the other party.

She shows insight and tact as she continues in this letter to ask the Earl if he will accommodate Henry and his wife in London.

I beseech you bring my Uncle Henry and my Aunt Grace with you up to London. They shall not long be troublesome to you, God willing; but because I know my uncle hath some very great occasion to be about London for a little while, and is not well able to bear his own charges, nor I for him, as I would very willingly if I was able, to so good an end as I know he comes to now. And therefore I beseech you take that pains and trouble of bringing them up. And keeping them awhile for my sake and our family's good. I have here enclosed sent you a letter to him, which if you grant him this favour I require of you, I beseech you send him, if you will not return it to me, and let him not be so much discomforted to see I am not able to obtain so much of you for him.[12]

Arbella always showed great wisdom and kindness in dealing with her friends when not suffering from the mental derangement caused by her illness. Most of the family troubles came from the fact that Bess had persuaded all four of her husbands to make her their heiress, to the detriment of the claims of their children. Both the Earl and Charles Cavendish were deeply in debt, and lawsuits were pending between Charles and Bess, which included Henry, hence his wish to visit London, most probably to consult lawyers. Sir William Stewart and Cook, the Earl's steward in London, both wrote to the family to tell them how hard Arbella was working on their behalf at court. Apparently the dispute between the Earl and Bess involved a great deal of money – in the region of £4,000. Cook wrote of Arbella's position as mediator: 'Surely she seems to have mastered them all that limited her before. I have never seen her ladyship more cheerful.' He asked the Earl on her behalf if she could have a room in his house in Broad Street. 'For although she be most resolute not to lodge from Court, yet she may have occasion for such a room.'

On 15 March, Arbella's exalted position at court was made public when, in the royal procession from the Tower of London to Whitehall, richly clothed on a velvet caparisoned horse, she rode at the Queen's side. In March she was given the prestigious position of Queen's Carver, In a letter to the Earl she tells him that she is feeling better but ruefully describes how she made a mess of her first attempt at carving. 'After I had once carved, the Queen never dined out of her bedchamber, nor was attended by any but her chamberers till my Lady of Bedford's return. I doubted my unhandsome carving had been the cause thereof, but her Majesty took my endeavour in good part, and with better words than that beginning deserved put me out of my error.'[13]

Arbella's great popularity with the King and Queen and her powerful position at court aroused the jealousy of the bickering court ladies. It needed all her tact and dignity to cope with it. The Earl of Worcester wrote: 'The plotting and malice among them is such that I think envy and malice and hatred hath tied an invisible snake around their necks to sting one another to death.'

That summer the King insisted on the court spending a great deal of time at Royston, where the hunting was excellent but the accommodation grim. He insisted that the court accompany him in his sport for many hours a day. The Earl of Worcester complained bitterly. 'In the mornings we are on horseback by eight in the morning, and so continue from the death of one hare to another, until four at night, then for the most part we are five miles from home.' Although an excellent horsewoman, Arbella hated the damp weather and found the exercise too much, and her health began to deteriorate again. In an undated letter to her aunt she wrote, 'Madame, this everlasting hunting, the toothache, and the continual means by my Lord Cecil to send to you, makes me only write these few lines to show I am not unmindful of your commandments, and reserve the rest I have to write, both to you and my uncle some few hours longer, till my pain assuage and I have given my never intermitted attendance on the Queen, who daily extends her favours more and more to me.'

It would seem that there was some slight disagreement between Arbella and her uncle and aunt, for there is quite a long gap in the letters, although she continued to work assiduously on her relatives' behalf, gaining a good position at court for Charles Cavendish as well as the resolution of the Earl's case against Bess.

During the year there were several suitors for Arbella's hand. The Queen's brother, Duke Ulric of Holstein, was one of them. He had been at court for some time and knew her well. Count Maurice, who pretended to be the Duke of Guelders, was another, as was the Prince of Anhault who wrote her lengthy, learned letters. But Arbella was not interested in any of them, and the King refused to give her permission to wed. James seemed to be as much against Arbella marrying as Queen Elizabeth had been, even though he had two sons and a daughter, so there was no danger of him dying without an heir. However, the contentious issue of marriage apart, he remained very attached to Arbella and, indeed, in December was to increase her allowance from £800 a year to £1,000.

FIRST LADY OF THE COURT

In December 1604 Arbella was ill again with a severe skin condition and living in seclusion at Sheffield Lodge with her uncle and aunt. In the light of her medical history, it seems likely that she was suffering from the skin symptoms of variegate porphyria, which could be mistaken for smallpox or measles and which consisted of a blotchy red rash on the face aggravated by being in the sun. Indeed, the Earl, writing to Cecil, stated that Arbella had had measles but was recovering. Although very weak she was fit to return to the court for Christmas but was unable to take part in any of the masques and revels – which may not have upset her unduly. The little Prince Charles, who had been brought down from Scotland, was at the Twelfth Night celebrations when he was made Duke of Albany and knighted with several other little boys. Five years old, he was too frail to walk and was carried throughout the ceremonies by the Lord Admiral. Arbella, always short of money, would have been relieved at the royal decision not to give New Year presents this year, as this custom had always been a great drain on her finances.

James went to Royston again to hunt in the New Year, but the Queen's entourage were allowed to remain behind because she was pregnant. Anne gave birth to a daughter on 6 April, the child being named Mary after James's mother. Arbella was asked to be godmother to the little girl, and the christening was arranged for early May.

Bess thought this was the moment to press for a barony for her beloved son William and expected Arbella to use her influence with the King to obtain one for him. William was a mean, grasping man and loath to hand out the usual large sums of money for such an honour. Arbella, who had never liked him, did not feel moved to put herself out for him, although he came to court and pleaded with her to assist him. The Earl of Worcester, writing to her uncle on 27 April, mentioned the new peers who were to be created at the infant's christening. He stated that the King had given Arbella a patent for whom she wished, leaving the name blank, 'to be created either then or hereafter to be named and created at her pleasure'. Before anything was decided about William, Bess became very ill and Arbella felt that she must ride up to Hardwick to see her. Remembering her last days at Hardwick, Arbella confided in the King her fears about what kind of reception she might receive. As a favour to her, James wrote a letter to Bess – one that annoyed her very much – telling her to receive Arbella with her former bounty and love.

Arbella arrived at Hardwick in April, and Bess, complying with the King's wishes, gave her a gold cup and £300. This did not prevent her from writing a waspish letter to Dr James Montague, Dean of the Royal Chapel, to be read to the King, revealing her real feelings about the visit. Montague was her confidant and kept her in close touch with affairs at court.

> It was very strange [she wrote] that my Lady Arbell should come to me with a recommendation as either doubting of her entertainment or desiring to come to her from who she had desired so earnestly to come away. That for her part she thought that she had sufficiently expressed her good meaning and kindness to her that had purchased her seven hundred pounds by year land of inheritance, and given her as much money as would buy one hundred pound by year more. And though for her part she had done very well for her according to her poor ability, yet she should be always welcome to her, though she had divers grandchildren that stood more in need than she, and much the more welcome in respect of the King's recommendation; she had bestowed on Arbella a cup of gold worth a hundred pounds, and three hundred pounds in money which deserved thankfulness very well, considering her poor ability.[1]

The Dean reported back that the King had laughed at the letter, which did not improve Bess's temper. Any attempts Arbella might have made to try to patch up the quarrel between the Shrewsburys and her grandmother was cut short by her having to return in time for the christening of Princess Mary in early May. William, to Bess's great joy, was made a baron at the christening; whether it was under Arbella's patent is not clear, but it seems likely. The ceremony was a magnificent affair. The Countess of Northumberland was the other godmother, Arbella's former rejected suitors, Duke Ulric and Esmé Stuart, now Duke of Lennox, were godfathers and William a canopy-holder for the little princess. Her funeral two years later was a cheap, plain affair, in stark contrast to her christening. Like her grandmother she was buried in Henry VII's Chapel in Westminster Abbey.

These happy days for Arbella as court favourite were enhanced by her friendship with Prince Henry. He was nineteen years younger than she, being nine years old when they first met, but Arbella became very fond of him, looking on him as a younger brother. He was equally delighted with her company, which compensated somewhat for his sorrow at parting from his young sister Elizabeth, who on their arrival in England had gone to live at Coombe Abbey in the charge of Lord and Lady Harrington.

Prince Henry was an attractive young boy. Intelligent without being intellectual, he admired the scholarship of his cousin. Even at a young age he had beautiful manners and, like Arbella, hated the crude behaviour of so many of his father's courtiers. James deplored his lack of scholarship and grew jealous of his growing popularity with his subjects. He was a fine horseman but did not share his father's passion for hunting.

Of the correspondence between Arbella and Henry, only two letters survive. He had obviously done her some favour, as she wrote to thank him in a letter written from London on 18 October 1605:

Sir, – My intention to attend your Highness tomorrow, God willing, cannot stay me from acknowledging, by these few lines, how infinitely I am bound to your Highness for that your gracious disposition towards me, which faileth not to show itself on every occasion, whether accidental or begging by me, as this late high favour and grace it hath pleased your Highness to do my kinsman at my humble suit. I trust tomorrow to let your Highness understand such motives of that my presumption as shall make it excusable. For your Highness shall perceive, I both understand with what extraordinary respects suits are to be presented to your Highness, and withal that your goodness doth so temper your greatness as it encourages both me and many others to hope that we may taste the fruits of the one by means of the other . . . And so in all humility I cease. Your Highness's most humble and dutiful Arbella Stuart.[2]

As the Shrewsburys were at court with her in 1606 there is no correspondence between them during that period. The Gunpowder Plot had been exposed in November the previous year, and we know that Arbella took a great interest in the affair, and when Father Garnet, who had acted as confessor to some of the conspirators, was bought to trial at the Guildhall on 28 March 1606 the King was there and many members of his court, including Arbella. The plot had made a deep impression on the King and his family, and if it had succeeded Arbella would have found herself a very strong candidate for the throne, even if the sickly Charles survived.

The Queen's brother, King Christian IV of Denmark, came to England to visit his sister in July 1606. This entailed more heavy expense for Arbella, as she had to be decked out in sumptuous clothes for the occasion as first lady of the court. The Queen gave birth to another daughter in April, Sophia, who died the same day, but Anne was very ill afterwards and was unable to greet her brother when he arrived. He called on his sister and her ladies in Greenwich, where he met Arbella and was very much taken with her. The absence of the Queen and her entourage meant that the two Kings spent several weeks in debauchery and drunken revelry, which Arbella was thankful to be able to avoid. The Queen was well enough to go to court in August, by which time King Christian's fondness for Arbella had grown, not least because, being an excellent linguist, she was able to speak to him a little in Danish.

Christian had an English chamberlain, Sir Andrew Sinclair, and Arbella carried on a correspondence with the King through him after he left England. She had embroidered a present for his wife and wrote a letter to the King to accompany it.

It may please you now with most humble thanks to present this letter to his Majesty, for whose prosperity none doth more daily and devoutly pray than I, and this work to the Queen's Majesty, which is so very a trifle, as I was ashamed to accompany it with a letter to Her Majesty, and if a piece of work of mine own, which I was preparing, had been ready, I had prevented his Majesty's gracious, and your kind letter in sending to you, but I was desirous not to omit her Majesty in the acknowledgement of my duty to her royal husband, and therefore loath to stay the finishing of a greater, have sent this little piece of work, in acceptance whereof her Majesty's favour will be the greater. Thus am I bold to trouble you with these womanish toys, whose serious mind must have some relaxation and this may be one to vouchsafe to descend to these petty offices for one that will ever wish you happiness to increase and continuance of honour.[3]

In his reply to Arbella on behalf of the King and Queen. Sir Andrew Sinclair wrote:

> The Queen, in especially, esteems much of that present your ladyship has sent her Majesty, and says that her Majesty will wear it for your ladyship's sake. The King has commanded me to assure your ladyship that there is no honour, advancement nor pleasure that his Majesty can do your lady-ship, but he shall do it, faithfully and willingly, as one of the best friends your ladyship has in the world. Surely I must confess with verity I never heard no prince speak more worthily of a princess than his Majesty does of your ladyship's good qualities and rare virtues, while I say no more, but I shall be a faithful instrument to entertain that holy friendship between his Majesty and your ladyship.[4]

There had been some misunderstanding between the King and Lady Nottingham, one of Arbella's relatives. Lord Nottingham was in com-mand of the ship that took him back to Denmark, and Lady Notting-ham, not speaking any Danish, had wrongly thought he had made a vulgar gesture to her. She wrote in a rage to him, and Arbella managed to diffuse the situation, much to the gratitude of Christian and Sinclair.

Early in 1607 Arbella was at Sheffield again, recovering from another bout of illness. It would appear from Queen Anne's coldness to her that she had offended her in some way, which may have triggered off another attack of porphyria; alternatively, she may have felt that the onset of illness made her a poor companion for the Queen. Her devotion to the Danish King was sorely tried when Anne wrote to her to say that her brother had taken a great liking for Arbella's brilliant lutist, Francis 'Thomas' Cutting, and asked if he could be sent to Denmark. The Queen wrote:

> Well beloved cousin – We greet you heartily well. Udo Gal, our dear brother's the King of Denmark's servant, hath insisted with us for the licensing your servant, Thomas Cutting, to depart from you, but not with-out your permission, to our brother's service; and therefore we write these few lines unto you, being assured you will make no difficulty to

satisfy our pleasure and our dear brother's desires, and so giving you the assurance of our constant favours, with our wishes for the continuance or convalescence of your health. Expecting your return, we commit you to the protection of God. March 9th, 1607.[5]

Poor Arbella had little choice but to comply with this request, especially as it was endorsed by a letter from Prince Henry, who wrote:

Madame, The Queen's Majesty hath commanded me to signify to your ladyship that she would have Cutting, your ladyship's servant, to send to the King of Denmark, because he desired the Queen that she would send him one that could play upon the lute. I pray your ladyship to send him back with an answer as soon as your ladyship can. I desire you to commend me to my Lord and Lady Shrewsbury; and also not to think me anything the worse scrivener that I write so ill, but to suspend your judgement till you come hither, when you shall find as I was ever, Your ladyship's most loving cousin and assured friend, Henry.[6]

His letter is certainly more cordial in tone than the Queen's, and he evidently did not relish the assistance the Queen had demanded of him. The musician was duly sent to Denmark, and Arbella in a short reply to the Queen makes it clear that, although she has agreed to part with him, it has been very hard for her to lose such a fine musician. Cutting was indeed considered one of the greatest musicians of the age, and his loss to Arbella was keen, although he did not stay in Denmark for very long, as in 1610 he appears again in England in the household of Prince Henry. Arbella wrote to Henry on 15 March 1607, the same day as she wrote to the Queen.

I have received your Highness's letter wherein I am let to understand that her royal Majesty is pleased to command Cutting my servant, for the King of Denmark, concerning the which your Highness requested my answer to her Majesty, the which I have accordingly returned by this bearer, referring him to her Majesty's good pleasure and disposition. And although I may have seen cause to be sorry to have lost the contentment of a good lute, yet must I confess that I am right glad to have found any occasion whereby to express to her Majesty and your Highness the humble respect which I owe you, and the readiness of my disposition to

be conformed to your good pleasures, wherein I have placed a great part
of the satisfaction which my heart can receive.[7]

At the age of thirty-two Arbella remained unmarried. Although she
had many suitors, James's refusal to let her marry without his consent
had not especially troubled her so far, and she had had four very happy
years at court as a favourite. But as she grew older her financial position
was becoming increasingly parlous. This, coupled with her recurrent
bouts of illness, relieved only by long stays in the private houses of her
relatives, made her long for a home of her own.

Young William Seymour, whose name had been coupled with hers
even as a boy prior to her departure from Hardwick, had developed into
a keenly intelligent, learned young man. He was sent to Magdalen College, Oxford, with his elder brother, where he graduated in 1605 at the
age of seventeen. Arbella probably met William during her stay with the
court at Woodstock, when many visits to Oxford were made. That they
became friends and enjoyed each other's company is not surprising,
despite the considerable difference in age.

The winter of 1607–8 was exceptionally harsh, with the Thames
frozen up for three months; during this time it became a solid road of ice
which could be traversed by wagons and carriages. During the cold
weather Arbella was grateful for the venison pasties which Gilbert
Shrewsbury sent her at frequent intervals. Extravagant masques were
held indoors, with the main performers being the Queen, Arbella and
her cousin the Countess of Arundel. The lavish costumes this involved,
encrusted with jewels, were another sore burden on her finances, and
debts continued to mount. Although the King joined in the revelry, he
soon tired of it and went to Theobalds, just north of London, shortly
afterwards, a house he had exchanged with Robert Cecil for Hatfield.

On 13 February 1608 Arbella was called away from court life by the
sudden death of her grandmother. In the last months of her life Bess
had made up her quarrels with her offspring, and they were all in attendance when she died. To show her gratitude to Arbella for her help in
getting William his peerage Bess left her the sum of £1,000. Although
the date on Bess's coffin is 16 February, she was not buried until the end
of April in All Hallows Church, Derby.

As soon as Bess was dead quarrels broke out among the children.
The Shrewsburys were disgusted by the behaviour of William, who took

charge of Hardwick even before his mother's will had been read. With Charles Cavendish they returned to Sheffield where Arbella joined them. It would appear that once again she was not very well, as the Earl wrote to Cecil that Arbella was 'ill at ease'. William meanwhile invited her to Hardwick, presumably still feeling indebted to her for his peerage. She went but only for a very short time. She wrote to her aunt on the night of her departure to thank her for her kind hospitality, not only after the death of her grandmother but on so many occasions.

Madame – I humbly thank you for your letters. I deferred to write to you till I had taken my leave here, and then I intended to have sent one to your ladyship and my uncle, to deliver my humble thanks for so many kindnesses and favours that I have received at this time of my being here from you both, and to take a more mannerly farewell than I could at our parting; but your ladyship hath prevented my intention in sending this bearer, by whom in these few lines, I will perform that duty of acknowledging myself bound to you for every particular kindness and bounty of yours at this time, which reviveth the memory of many former.[8]

She was back in London by 23 March, when her name was mentioned in the marriage between William's young son and the daughter of Lord Kinloss, Master of the Rolls. They were married secretly in the Chapel of the Rolls, and a large family dinner was held afterwards which Arbella attended.

At Michaelmas 1608 Arbella bought herself a residence at Blackfriars for £200. This was a desirable area just outside the City, enclosed by the walls of a Dominican priory. A theatre stood near by, restored by the Burbage family. It was very close to here that Arbella was to be placed under house arrest with Sir Thomas Parry at Copt Hall two years later.

There is little record of her activities during the rest of this year apart from requests from her to James for some monopolies on oats, which he granted but which she never received. Her income at this time was £2,160 a year, nothing like enough for her to maintain her position at court. On 8 December she wrote to the Earl sending him some cheese and salad in return for venison pies. Much of the letter makes little or no sense, so it is not surprising that on 21 December Sir John Harrington wrote to a friend to say that Arbella had been taken very ill. He describes the illness as smallpox, but any disease accompanied by a rash on the face was always so described, so it is much more likely that she had suffered another attack of porphyria, She was put into the care of Lady Skinner, and her sickness lasted until February 1609. We know this because on the 2nd of that month she was back at court at Whitehall in time for Candlemas and was well enough to take part in a performance of Ben Jonson's *Masque of Queens*.

The clouds were beginning to gather around her, however. James was becoming weary of her endless demands for money and may have been watching with some alarm her developing friendship with William Seymour. Her illness may have made her difficult and irascible, and her distaste for the more frivolous aspects of court life might have been becoming evident. She decided to get away from it all by going on a royal progress of her relatives and friends. The expenses of the trip were itemized in great detail by her steward Mr Hugh Crompton.[9]

She left Whitehall on Tuesday 22 August and slept the first night at St Albans. The next stop was with Lady Cheneys at Toddington, near Dunstable. On Saturday the 26th she went via Northampton to Prestwood to the house of Sir William Skipwith. She then visited her good friend Lady Bowes at Walton Hall near Chesterfield. The latter had been married first to Godfrey Foljambe and later to Sir William Bowes, whose descendants married into the family of the Earls of Strathmore, incorporating their name with his. (In 1617, after Arbella's death, Lady Bowes married Lord Darcy, one of Arbella's hosts on her royal progress.) Arbella stayed at Walton Hall until 2 September, when she moved on to Sheffield. Here she was received with great pomp by her relatives, who offered her lavish hospitality. Her next stop was at Melwood Park, South Yorkshire, as the guest of Sir George St Paul. She stayed with him for four days and then went to Aston, near Sheffield, to the house of Lord Darcy, for one night. Sunday 17 September was spent at Chatsworth, and from there she went to Buxton to take the waters, returning to Sheffield on the 20th. Next she visited Rufford with her aunt, where her parents had married, spending the night at the house of George Markham. From there she went to Wingfield where she had many memories of her childhood days with Mary Queen of Scots. Her next stop on the homeward journey was Quarndon Manor, the home of the Farnham family, near Loughborough. Following this she stayed at Easton Maudit, near Wellingborough, the house of Sir Christopher Yelverton for two days, moving on to visit her favourite cousins, the Kents, at Wrest House, which had proved such a haven after leaving her grandmother. She remained with them for six days before finally returning to London.

The progress turned out to be very expensive, with generous gifts being bestowed on friends, relatives and servants, as well as the not inconsiderable cost of replacing horses and repairing carriages. The total came to £323 18s, not including the extra bills that came later and interest on money borrowed for the journey on the security of jewels. However, expense apart, the progress was a great personal success for Arbella. She was greeted in her own home county with many gifts and the ringing of church bells in Sheffield. The journey was to have a profound effect upon her, making her long for a more settled life that only marriage could confer.

Arbella Stuart as a young woman; engraving by J.G. Stoddart, from a contemporary miniature, originally in the Hammond Collection, its whereabouts now unknown

The Memorial of Lord Darnley, 1567, by Livinus de Vogelaare. The future James I of England kneels beside the tomb of his father; behind him are his grandparents, the Earl and Countess of Lennox, and their younger son, Charles Stuart, Arbella's father. Lord Darnley was murdered in 1567, aged twenty-two.

Lord Darnley, aged seventeen, husband of Mary Queen of Scots and father of James I; with his brother Charles Stuart, aged six, who became Earl of Lennox, married Bess of Hardwick's daughter, Elizabeth Cavendish, and was the father of Arbella Stuart.

Elizabeth Talbot, Countess of Shrewsbury
(Bess of Hardwick), maternal grandmother of
Arbella Stuart and her guardian after the death
of her mother, Elizabeth Cavendish, Countess
of Lennox. This portrait was painted in 1581.

View of Old Chatsworth, 1680, birthplace of Arbella Stuart;
painted by R. Wilson (after Siberechts)

Portrait of Lady Margaret Douglas, Countess of Lennox, paternal grandmother to Arbella Stuart; artist unknown. She was the daughter of Henry VIII's eldest sister, Margaret, and Archibald, 6th Earl of Angus, and the granddaughter of Henry VII.

Lady Arbella Stuart, aged twenty-three months; artist unknown. The portrait gives her the title Countess of Lennox, one her grandmother, Bess of Hardwick, tried unsuccessfully to establish for her after the death of the Earl of Lennox. The doll bears a resemblance to Elizabeth I.

Hardwick Hall, home of Arbella Stuart until 1603, as it appears today

© English Heritage

The Ceremonial Staircase

The High Great Chamber

Enamel miniature of Mary Queen of Scots; one of the few portraits to show her beauty and charm

© Inverness Museum and Art Gallery

Engraving of Sir Walter Mildmay, Chancellor of the Exchequer to Elizabeth I. Sir Walter met Arbella several times as a young girl on his visits to Mary Queen of Scots during her captivity in various Shrewsbury houses in Derbyshire.

Above: Wingfield Manor, Derbyshire, one of the houses belonging to the Shrewsburys where Mary Queen of Scots was held prisoner, with the young Arbella Stuart as a frequent companion

Left: Lady Arbella Stuart, aged thirteen; English School, 1589

© Devonshire Collection (National Trust)

Below: Queen Mary's Bower at Chatsworth, as it appears today. Mary Queen of Scots spent many hours here, heavily guarded and accompanied by Arbella.

James I of England, Arbella's first cousin; portrait attributed to De Critz and now in a private collection

© Photographic Survey, Courtauld Institute of Art

James's wife, Anne of Denmark; portrait after Van Somer and now in a private collection

© Photographic Survey, Courtauld Institute of Art

134

My good Lord. / I humbly thanck your Lo.p
for procuring and hastening the Kings liberality
towards me. I acknowledge my selfe greatly bounde
to your Lo.p and haue sent this bearer my seruant
to attend your pleasure, whose important affaires
I am constrained to interrupt wth this necessary
importunity. And so wishing your Lo.p all honour
and contentment I recomend you to the protection
of the Almighty. From Sheene the 26 of Iune
1603

Your Lo:ps poore frend. /

Arbella Stuart.

Letter from Arbella to Lord Cecil, 26 June 1603. This shows her excellent handwriting which
deteriorated during her bouts of illness.

Lady Arbella Stuart; attributed to Robert Peake, Serjeant Painter to James I. This portrait of Arbella shows her probably towards the end of her life, in her mid-thirties.

Reproduced by permission of the Scottish National Portrait Gallery

William Seymour, from an engraving of an original portrait in Badminton House. A man of great integrity, after his marriage to Arbella he fled into exile, returning to England only after her death. He became a trusted statesman to Charles I and Charles II, who on the Restoration created him Duke of Somerset.

Reproduced by kind permission of the Royal Geographical Society

Sir Theodore Turquet de Mayerne by Rubens. Dr Mayerne was appointed First Physician to James I in 1611. He was a gifted doctor who devoted himself to minute clinical observance of his patients. His detailed medical notes on the illnesses of James I and Prince Henry led to a diagnosis of porphyria three centuries later.

© British Museum

Prince Henry, eldest son of James I and first cousin once removed to Arbella; copy of a portrait by Daniel Mytens, 1627, of a miniature by Isaac Oliver, 1612. In spite of his and Arbella's difference in age, they became close friends.

Reproduced by kind permission of the Hon. Jeremy Addington

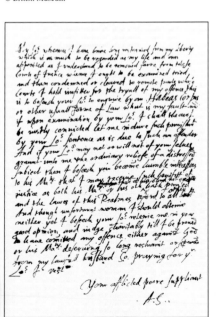

Draft letter of Arbella Seymour from Copt Hall to the Lord Chief Justice of England and the Lord Chief Justice of the Common Pleas, March 1610. The erratic handwriting reveals the distress she felt on being told she was to be transferred to the care of the Bishop of Durham, which meant she would not see her husband again.

© The Marquess of Salisbury

Above: The chamber in the Bell Tower of the
Tower of London, where Arbella is said to have
been kept prisoner until her death

Right: Lady Arbella's burial place. The tomb of
Mary Queen of Scots in Henry VII's Chapel,
Westminster Abbey. Arbella shares this tomb
with Mary and Prince Henry. A small stone slab
on the floor is the only memorial.

LADY ARBELLA SEYMOUR

During her royal progress Arbella seems to have discussed with Isobel, Lady Bowes, the matter of acquiring another house of her own in the country.

Worries about Arbella's health continued, and on her return from the progress, according to an undated letter to her aunt, she suffered another bad bout of neuralgia. Arbella had asked Cecil to arrange with the King her right to sell wines in Ireland, and she wrote to him on 17 December 1609 asking for his confirmation of this. For some reason she appears to have suddenly changed her mind and asked him in an interview if in exchange for renouncing her licence for the Irish wines she might have her debts paid and an increased allowance granted from the King. She also said that she would prefer £1,000 a year instead of the diet allowance from the King's table. It was obvious that she was seriously contemplating marriage and the acquisition of a country estate of her own. Cecil was shocked and asked her to petition the King in writing, which she duly did.

> Dec. 1609. Where your Lordship willed me to set down a note of those three things wherein I lately moved you, they are these: The first, that I am willing to return back His Majesty's gracious grant to me of the wines in Ireland, so as your Lordship will take order for the paying of my debts, when I shall upon mine honour inform you truly what they are. The next that his Majesty will be graciously pleased to augment my allowance in such sort as I may be able to live in such honour and countenance hereafter as may stand with His Majesty's honour and my own comfort. And lastly that his Majesty doth now allow me a diet, that he will be pleased, instead thereof, to let me have one thousand pounds yearly. Some other things I will presume to entreat your Lordship's like favour in that they may stand me in stead; but, for that they are such as I trust your Lordship will think his Majesty will easily grant, I will now forbear to set them down. Your lordship's poor friend Arbella Stuart.[1]

A few days later Arbella was arrested. The only information we have about this is in a letter from John Chamberlain, written on 30 December. 'I can learn no more of the Lady Arbella, but that she is committed to the Lady Knyvett, and was yet again before the Lords. Her gentleman usher and her waiting-woman are close prisoners since her restraint.'[2] Lady Kynevet's husband was a justice of the peace of Westminster and a privy councillor, who had a house in King's Street, Westminster. It was he who had discovered the gunpowder on 4 November beneath the House of Commons and who afterwards heard the confession of Guy Fawkes.

Arbella had obviously made up her mind to marry but without telling anyone that William Seymour was the object of her affections. Rumours were flying about at this time, connecting her name with various foreign princes, in particular the Prince of Moldavia, but she gave nothing away under questioning from the Council,

The King was horrified at the idea of her marrying a foreigner and, since she realized that this was why she had been arrested, she kept silent about William, simply making a solemn promise not to marry a foreigner. In return Arbella received James's permission to take as her husband any man she pleased so long as he was a loyal subject of the realm. She was immediately restored to favour, and she decided not to press for the increases in her income. On 20 January, however, a warrant was signed for her diet, an addition of £600 a year to her income, 1,000 marks (a mark was valued at two-thirds of a pound) to pay her debts and £200 worth of plate as a New Year's gift. This was generous of James, and it was obvious that he had not the slightest idea of her intention to marry into the Hertford family.

From the moment he succeeded to the English throne James had proved a loving cousin and a staunch and generous friend to Arbella, and she, in turn, had also grown very close to the young Prince Henry. The dramatic deterioration in their relationship with her – which became evident soon after this – seems out of all proportion to her wish to marry into the Seymour family, even though they had fallen out of favour with the King. James, after all, had two sons and a daughter in direct line to the throne, Arbella's claim coming into force only if all of them died. It seems, however, that not long after Arbella undertook not to marry a foreigner the King discovered the true object of his cousin's affections and was grievously affected by this knowledge.

One perhaps needs to consider James's mental state at this time to understand his violent change in attitude towards Arbella. Meticulous medical notes were made by his personal physician, the celebrated Dr Mayerne – who arrived in England from Paris in 1610 to take over the King's medical care – and they provide a detailed description of James's mysterious ailments, which we now know to be typical of porphyria.[3] He suffered abdominal pain, accompanied by vomiting and diarrhoea, changes in mood, 'melancholy', fits of unconsciousness and delirium, pain and weakness in the limbs, insomnia, respiratory difficulties, sensitivity to sunlight, skin fragility and production of dark urine, which the King described as the colour of Alicante wine. In the summer of 1611 James became so overheated that his face, particularly his forehead, broke out into a vesicular rash, followed by violent headaches, vomiting and acute pain. His vomiting was persistent and uncontrollable, with turbulent nights when he became delirious and was subject to hallucinations. Dr Mayerne was terrified that he had water on the brain.

So it seems that James had a severe attack in 1610 and another in 1611, with major mental disturbance as well as physical symptoms. He suffered from a third serious attack in 1612 after the death of Prince Henry. He was a very poor sleeper and easily disturbed, and the attacks were apparently brought on by 'anxiety, sadness and cold at night'. Arbella's symptoms were also exacerbated by stress, worry and extreme cold. It seems highly likely therefore that James and Arbella were suffering from the same disease. It was Arbella's fate that her decision to marry coincided with severe attacks of porphyria in James and may well account for his unduly harsh treatment of her after the kindness and tolerance he had shown her hitherto. And indeed it was his savage treatment of her that triggered the disease in her once more.

When Arbella had an attack of the illness it tended to make her intolerant and unreasonable, and she would have been in no frame of mind to placate the ailing King and persuade him to agree to her marriage. As we have seen, Arbella when ill was quite incapable of coping with a difficult situation, and James's irrational fury at Arbella's plans points to him suffering from the same illness.

James, a clever man, had already recognized his symptoms as similar to those suffered by his mother.[4] One can but speculate whether he recognized the same symptoms in Arbella and, two years later, in his eldest son. Whether he did or not, it did not stop Arbella falling out of favour with him.

The King's granting of permission for her to marry 'a loyal British subject of her choice' had naturally encouraged William and Arbella to be more open about their attachment to each other. They were obviously very well suited, as neither enjoyed the frivolity, extravagance and raucous horseplay at court. They both loved studying and spent as much time as possible with their books. In her mid-thirties she was still an attractive woman, and he delighted in her company. In choosing him as her future husband, Arbella had found an ideal partner. Clarendon described him as 'a man of great honour, interest and estate. He was a man of very good parts, and conversant in books both in Latin and Greek languages, and of a clear courage.' He was, as his subsequent life reveals, a worthy husband for her, and it was tragic that they were to spend such a short time together.

On 2 February 1610 William went to Arbella's room and asked her to marry him, and they went through some kind of formal betrothal ceremony. They had two more meetings within the next few days at the houses of friends, Mr Buggs of Fleet Street and Mr Baynton. Having made little or no attempt to keep the affair secret, the news soon reached the King. Thanks to Dr Mayerne's medical notes, we know that James had a difficult time with Parliament in February, when the members discussed his favourites and refused him the subsidies he wanted, so he dissolved it on the 11th in a rage and was taken very ill immediately afterwards. The medical report states that 'after great sadness' he had diarrhoea for eight days, 'with watery bilious, very fetid and at last black excreta. Cardialgia, palpitations, sighing, sadness, etc. Vomiting recurring twice or thrice a day.' James seems to have been in the middle of a serious attack of porphyria when he heard the news about Arbella and William. Furious, he had them both arrested and brought before the Council.

On 15 February James Beaulieu, secretary to the diplomat Sir Thomas Edmondes, wrote a waspish letter to William Trumbull, British Resident at Brussels.

> The Lady Arbella who (as you know) was not long ago censured for having without the King's privity, entertained a motion of marriage, was again within these few days apprehended in the like treaty with the Lord Beauchamp's second son, and both were called and examined yesterday

at the Court about it. What the matter will prove I know not, but these affections of marriage do give some advantage to the world of impairing the reputation of her constant and virtuous disposition.[5]

William wrote a formal submission about the affair on 20 February. It is extremely cautious, explaining that neither he nor Arbella would contemplate marriage without the King's permission. He also diplomatically pointed out what an advantageous marriage it would be for him. Having been reared in a family that was out of favour with the court, he was obviously doing his best to placate the King. His submission in its entirety runs as follows:

To the Right Honourable my most singular good Lords, the Lords of His Majesty's Most Honourable Privy Council. May it please your Lordships: Since it is your pleasure, which for me will always stand for law, that I should truly relate under my hand those passages that have been between the noble Lady Arbella and myself, I do here, in these rugged lines, truly present the same to your Lordships' favourable censure, that thereby his most excellent Majesty may, by your Lordships, be fully satisfied of my duty and faithful allegiance (which shall ever be a spur to me to expose my life and all my fortunes to the extremest dangers for his Highness's service), and that I will never attempt anything which I shall have certain foreknowledge will be displeasing to him.

I do therefore confess that when I conceived that noble lady might, with his Majesty's good favour, and no just offence make her choice of any subject within this kingdom, which conceit was begotten in me upon a general report, after her ladyship last being called before your Lordships that it might be; myself being a younger brother, and sensible of my own good, unknown to the world, of mean estate, not born to challenge anything by my birthright, and therefore my fortunes to be raised by mine own endeavours, and she a lady of great honour and virtue, and as I thought, of great means, I did plainly and honestly endeavour lawfully to gain her in marriage, which is God's ordinance common to all, assuming myself, if I could affect the same with His Majesty's most gracious favour and liking (without which I resolved never to proceed), that thence would grow the first beginning of all my happiness; and therefore I boldly intruded myself into my lady's chamber in the court on Candlemas Day last, at what time I imparted my desire unto her; which was entertained, but with this caution on either part, that both of us resolved not to proceed to any final conclusion without His Majesty's most gracious favour and liking first obtained; and this was our first meeting. After that we had a second meeting at Mr Buggs's house, in Fleet Street; and then a third at Mr Baynton's; at both which we had the like conference and resolution as before. And the next day save one after the last meeting, I was convented before your Lordships, when I did then deliver as much as now I have written; both then and now protesting before God, upon my duty and allegiance to his most excellent Majesty, and as I desire to be retained in your Lordships' good opinions, there is neither promise of marriage, contract or any other engagement whatsoever between the lady and myself, nor never was there any marriage by me or her intended, unless his Majesty's gracious favour and approbation might have been gained therein, which we resolved to obtain before we would proceed to any final conclusion. Whereof I humbly beseech your Lordships to inform his Majesty by your own good means, joined to the clearness of an unspotted conscience, and a loyal heart to his Highness, I may be acquitted in his just judgement from all opinion of any disposition in me to attempt anything distasteful or displeasing to His Majesty as one well knowing that the just wrath and disfavour of my Sovereign will be my confusion, whereas his gracious favour and goodness towards me be the advancement of my poor fortunes. And thus my Lords according to your commands, I have made a true relation of what was required, humbly referring the favourable construction thereof to your Lordships, having for the further hastening of the truth, and ever to bind me thereunto, hereafter subscribe my name on the 20th February, 1610 William Seymour.[6]

The submission would have been written purely to protect Arbella from the King's wrath. Benjamin Disraeli wrote in 1838, 'There is nothing romantic in this apology in which Seymour describes himself as a fortune hunter, which, however, was undoubtedly done to cover his undoubted affection for Arbella, whom he had early known.'[7] There is a rough draft of an anonymous unsigned letter in the Longleat papers, discovered by Canon Jackson, librarian to the fourth Marquis of Bath in the mid nineteenth century, in which it is stated that William suggests that for Arbella's sake the engagement should be broken off. He would have recalled the terrible consequences of the marriage made by his grandfather to Catherine Grey and considered the consequences for Arbella if they went through with the marriage.

> I am come with a message to your Ladyship, which was delivered unto me in the presence of this gentleman your servant, and therefore your Ladyship may be assured I will neither add nor diminish, but will truly relate unto you, what he hath directed me to do, which is this. He hath seriously considered of the proceedings between your Ladyship and himself, and does well perceive, if he should go on therein, it would not only prove exceedingly prejudicial to your contentment, but extreme danger to him, first in regard to the inequality between your Ladyship and him, next the King's Majesty's pleasure and commandment to the contrary, which neither your Ladyship nor himself did ever intend to neglect. He doth therefore humbly desire your Ladyship, since the proceeding that is past does not tie him or your Ladyship to any necessity, but that you may freely commit each other to your best fortunes, that you would be pleased to desist from your intended resolution concerning him, who likewise resolveth not to trouble you any more in this kind, not doubting that your Ladyship may have one more fitting to your degree (he having already presumed too high) and himself a meaner match, with more security.[8]

Arbella was too much in love with Wiiliam to contemplate this course of action, however, and it was never mentioned again. William's submission seemed to have satisfied James, and he and Arbella were received back at court at the end of March, and the confirmation of her Irish wine monopoly was ratified.

So Arbella appeared to be much in the King's favour again, but James's continued hostility to a Hertford marriage for Arbella would have been aggravated by the extraordinary fact that after Elizabeth's death in 1603 – and James's succession – the legal right to the throne, according to the statutes then in force, was vested in William's father Edward Seymour, Lord Beauchamp, eldest son of the Earl of Hertford and Lady Catherine Grey. Because of the Alien Act, which stated that the heir to the throne had to be born on English soil, James's hereditary pretension to the throne was not acknowledged or ratified by Parliament until March 1604, a fact that he would find hard to forget.

After their return to court the two lovers managed to be fairly discreet about their affection for one other, but court gossip abounded about an impending marriage. The rumours reached Lord Dunfermline in Edinburgh, a close confidant of the Stuarts. He had been custodian of the young Prince Charles when he was left in Scotland after his father went to England to take the throne. He also controlled the property of the Queen when she travelled south to join her husband. He wrote to Salisbury on 31 March 1610 about the matter. Salisbury had been told by the King that if he was questioned about Arbella's and Seymour's relationship he was to deny it. 'We have much talk here', wrote Dunfermline, 'of Arbella's business here, but indeed amongst divers rumours of that matter the most constant report we had here was of her intention to have married to the younger son of Lord Beauchamp. This was written by sundry and by some who seemed to have responsible knowledge and intelligence of Arbella's affairs – a great argument not to give trust to reports in the matters of importance, for on light conjecture and weak ground strong assertions will be builded and go far ahead.'[9] The Earl had come south to visit the court in 1609 and would have met Arbella when he was made a member of the Privy Council. At any rate he evidently showed an interest in her.

As the months passed, William and Arbella appear to have decided that, even though James might initially be angry with them if they married in secret, they would soon be forgiven. Both of them were determined to wed, and William started making plans.

However, any plans for marriage that they might make had to be postponed until after the celebrations that accompanied Prince Henry being invested as Prince of Wales. Arbella was still on excellent terms with him at the time and must have taken a keen interest in the bequest he received in 1609 from the late Lord Lumley – who was childless – of his magnificent library. Henry installed it at St James's Palace, had it catalogued, which took nearly a year, and for the remainder of his life added to it himself. It was later to form the core of the collection in the British Library. A month before the investiture the French King Henry IV was assassinated, which came as an enormous shock to the Prince. He had been a great admirer of the King, and on hearing of his death he exclaimed, 'My second father is dead.'

The investiture took place on 4 June. James, always loath to spend money on his son, insisted that the royal party came to Westminster by water, which was much cheaper than a huge procession by road. John Hawkins describes the sixteen-year-old Prince at this time as 'comely, middle stature about five feet eight tall, of a strong, straight well-made body, with somewhat broad shoulders and a small waist, of an amiable majestic countenance, his hair of an auburn colour, long face, broad forehead, and a piercing grave eye, a most gracious smile and a most terrible frown'.[10]

The Queen presented a masque the following day – *Tethy's Festival*, in which Arbella took a leading role after the Queen and Princess Elizabeth. Her costume was breathtaking and cost a fortune:

Her head tire was composed of shells and coral, and from a great murex shell in the form of the crest of an helm, hung a thin waving veil. The upper garments had the boddies of sky coloured taffatoes, for lightness, all embroidered with maritime invention. Then had she a kind of half skirt of cloth of silver embroidered with gold, all the ground work cut out for lightness, which hung down full and cut into points. Underneath that came a base (of the same as was her body beneath her knee). Her long skirt was wrought with lace, waved round about like a river, and on the banks sedge and seaweed all of gold. Her shoulders were all embroidered with the work of the short skirt of cloth of silver, and had cypruss spangled, riffed out, and fell in a ruff above the elbow. The under sleeves were all embroidered as the boddies. Her shoes were of satin richly embroidered with the work of the short skirt.[11]

By this time the plans for the marriage had been carefully laid. William took into his confidence a cousin of his, Edward Rodney, even though Rodney was greatly disliked by William's grandfather, the Earl of Hertford, who considered him a dangerous and unsuitable friend for his grandson. Rodney gives his account of the pre-nuptial plans in the Declaration he was forced to make after the marriage was discovered.

About Whitsuntide meeting with Mr Seymour at Lambeth, among other speech which he used to me, it pleased him to acquaint me with his resolution concerning his marriage, but so sparingly and in such general terms, that he never spake unto me of the means, which he used in the reobtaining of her love, nor once mentioned unto me either Letter, Token or Message or aught else that had passed between them. Only that since it pleased her to entertain the matter, having the King's consent to make her own choice without exception, and since he found himself bound in conscience by reason of a former pledging of his faith unto her, that he resolutely intended it, engaging me by oath unto him that I should not reveal it, until he absolved me, and seeming to me to fear no other let or obstacle than his grandfather, my Lord of Hertford. From that time until the marriage day, he used no more words to me concerning it, at what time he requested me to accompany him to her chamber at Greenwich, to be a witness to his marriage there to be solemnised, to which I consented, all this while nothing doubting of the King's consent.[12]

On Thursday 21 June William went to Lambeth to fetch Rodney. Both men went by river to Greenwich Palace to the court and headed straight to Arbella's chamber. Four of her servants were assembled there, Kirton, Reeves, Mrs Biron and Mrs Bradshaw, who had been with her since 1603, and her gentleman usher and steward Hugh Crompton who left the only known written evidence of the marriage – apart from William's confession. This document was not to come to light until the 1850s when Canon Jackson accidentally came upon it in the Longleat papers.[13] The ceremony was performed at four in the morning by a Mr Blague, probably a contemporary of William's at Oxford. Crompton wrote on the flyleaf of his account book 'One Blague son of the Dean of Rochester was the minister that married them.'

THE HOUSE PRISONER

Neither William nor Arbella could have envisaged the tragic outcome of their secret wedding. Arbella would have remembered that the marriage of her parents without royal consent had meant the imprisonment in the Tower of London of both her grandmothers; William, likewise, would have known well the unhappy story of his grandfather's marriage to Catherine Grey. But they both expected that they would be forgiven in time. That this did not happen may have been a result of James's deteriorating health, which would have affected both his temper and his judgement, not to mention his fears for the succession if they had a child.

The news of the marriage had reached James by 8 July, just over two weeks after it had taken place and, as the couple had anticipated, they were immediately placed in custody, William in the Tower and Arbella under house arrest with Sir Thomas Parry at Lambeth. Her two servants, Crompton and Reeves, found themselves in parlous circumstances in the Marshalsea Prison, and the parson Blague was taken to the gatehouse at Westminster. The warrant sent to Parry for Arbella's custody ran as follows:

> After our very hearty commendations. Whereas it is thought fit that the Lady Arbella should be restrained of her liberty, and choice is made of you to receive and lodge her in your house – These are therefore to give you notice thereof, and to require you to provide convenient lodgings for her to remain under your charge and custody, with one or two of her women to attend her, without access of any other person until His Majesty's pleasure be further known. And this shall be unto you a sufficient warrant. From the Court at Whitehall, this 9th of July, 1610. Your very loving friends, R. Cant, T. Ellesmere, Nottingham, J. Suffolk, R. Salisbury, E. Worcester.[1]

Meanwhile Edward Rodney was summoned before the Privy Council where he made his declaration.[2]

Parry was the eldest son of Sir Thomas Parry, Comptroller of the Royal Household, and he was a kinsman of Sir William Cecil. He succeeded to the manor of Hampstead Marshall, Berkshire, and was appointed Ambassador to France by Elizabeth in 1601 and again by James in 1603. On his retirement from the post he was made Chancellor of the Duchy of Lancaster and a Privy Councillor. His house in Lambeth, Copt Hall, was on the River Thames near Vauxhall. It is described by John Norden, the sixteenth-century topographer, in his survey as 'a fair dwelling house, strongly built, three stories high, and a fair staircase breaking out of it 19 feet square'. It had a large garden in which Arbella was allowed to walk. She had her own set of apartments, women to wait on her, could correspond with her friends and was allowed any books and amusements she requested.

To be deprived of her life at court was no hardship to her, and her arrest was certainly not arduous. She was, without doubt, able to correspond with her husband, who was first lodged with the Lieutenant of the Tower, Sir William Waad, until he was able to furnish the grand apartments he was given in St Thomas's Tower above Traitor's Gate. They overlooked the river on one side and Raleigh's Walk on the other. He bought tapestries and, with Arbella's permission, sent for furnishing and plate and linen from her family home, then occupied by servants, at Hackney. His grandfather gave him an allowance and, with the King's consent, £50 for his maintenance. Indeed, although they were deprived of one another's company, both William and Arbella were comfortably housed and had a certain amount of freedom.

One of Arbella's main concerns was the plight of her servants. She wrote to her Uncle Gilbert in July from Lambeth on the matter.

If it please your lordship, there are divers of my servants with whom I thought never to have parted whilst I lived, and none that I am willing to part with. But since I am taken and know not how to maintain either myself or them, being utterly ignorant how it will please his Majesty to deal with me, I were better to put them away now than towards winter. Your lordship knows the greatness of my debts, and my unableness to do for them either now or at Michaelmas. I beseech your lordship let me know what hope you can give me of His Majesty's favour, without which I and all mine must live in great discomfort, and make me so much bound to you, as both yourself and by means of any that you take to be my friends or pity me, to labour the reobtaining of His Majesty's favour to me. So humbly thanking your lordship for the care it pleaseth you to have of me and mine, and for your honourable offer, I humbly cease. From Lambeth the 16th of July 1610. The poor prisoner your niece, Arbella Seymaure. P.S. The bay gelding and the rest are at your lordship's commandment.[3]

The Earl managed to dispose of some of her servants, but the plight of Crompton and Reeves in the Marshalsea was still a particular worry to her. On 10 August she wrote to the Privy Council:

I am constrained to trouble you rather than be guilty of the danger of life wherein Hugh Crompton and Edward Reeves, two of my servants, lately committed to the Marshalsea for my cause, remain. I am informed divers near that prison, and in it are lately dead, and divers others sick of contagious and deadly diseases. Wherefore I humbly beseech your honours to commiserate their distress, and consider that they are servants, and accountable for divers debts and reckonings, which, if they should die, would be a great prejudice to me and others. And therefore I humbly beseech you to move unto His Majesty my most humble suit and theirs, that it will please His Majesty they may be removed to some other healthful air.[4]

This letter was sent from Millbrook, presumably where some friends of hers lived, which suggests that Arbella had the freedom to leave Copt Hall from time to time.

Some time in July 1610 she wrote to the Privy Council:

Right Honourable and my very good Lords, I humbly beseech you give me leave to become a humble suitor to you to let His Majesty understand my hearty sorrow for His Majesty's displeasure and that it will please your Honours to become intercessors to His Majesty for me, whose error I assuredly hope His Majesty of his own gracious disposition will, by your good means, rather pardon than any further expiate with imprisonment or other affliction. Which and more, if it were to do His Majesty service or honour, I should endure with alacrity; but this is very grievous, especially as a sign of His Majesty's displeasure, on whose favour all my worldly joy as well as fortune dependeth. Which if I may reobtain, all the course of my life hereafter shall testify my dutiful and humble thankfulness. Arbella Seymaure.[5]

She wrote a short letter to the Queen on 23 July 1610 enclosing a small gift.

May it please your most excellent Majesty, since I am debarred the happiness of attending your Majesty, or so much as to kiss your Royal hands, to pardon my presumption in presenting your Majesty in this rude form my most humble thanks for your Majesty's gracious favour and mediation to your Majesty for me, which your Majesty's goodness (my greatest comfort and hope in this affliction) I most humbly beseech your Majesty to continue. So praying to the Almighty to reward your Majesty, with all honour and felicity, both in your royal self and yours, in all humility I cease. From Lambeth, the 23rd of July 1610, your Majesty's most humble and dutiful servant, Arbella Seymaure.[6]

She wrote again to the Queen in October, enclosing a petition to the King. The strain of her house arrest is obviously beginning to tell on her, and there are signs of the mental imbalance seen in her last letters from Hardwick. The strange notes written in her hand on the back of the letter are very odd: 'J'ai perdu ta successeur mais non pas tu' and 'La perte de ta soeur te portoit l'honneur d'être serviteur de ma belle fleur.'[7]

Her petition to the King is a forthright defence of herself and her marriage to William and shows a firm belief in its insolubility. The humble tone of her other petitions written at this time is absent.

May it please your most excellent Majesty. I do most heartily lament my hard fortune that I should offend your Majesty the least, especially in that whereby I have long desired to merit of your Majesty, as appeared before your Majesty was my sovereign. And though your Majesty's neglect of me, and my love to this gentleman that is my husband, and my fortune drove me to a contract before I acquainted your Majesty, I humbly beseech your Majesty to consider how impossible it was for me to imagine it would be offensive to your Majesty having a few days before given me leave to bestow myself on any subject of your Majesty, which likewise

your Majesty had done long since. Besides having never been prohibited
nor spoken to of any in this land by your Majesty these seven years that I
have lived in your Majesty's house, I could not conceive that your Majesty
regarded my marriage at all. And I protest if your Majesty had vouch-
safed to tell me your mind and to accept the freewill offering of my
obedience I would not have offended your Majesty, of whose gracious
goodness I presume so much that if it were as convenient in a worldly
respect as malice may make it seem to separate us whom God hath
joined, your Majesty would not do evil that good might come thereof, nor
make me that have the honour to be so near your Majesty in blood the
first precedent that ever was, although our own Princes may have left
some as little inimitable for so good and gracious a King as your Majesty
as David dealing with Uriah. But I assure myself that if it please your
Majesty in your own wisdom to consider thoroughly my cause, there will
no solid reason appear to debar me of justice and your princely favour
which I will endeavour to deserve whilst I breathe, and never ceasing to
pray for your Majesty's felicity in all things.[8]

Edward Rodney, who lodged in Lambeth with William's younger
brother Francis, would have been of considerable help in keeping him in
contact with his wife by passing on messages and delivering letters.
Arbella's cousin, Jane Drummond, a favourite of the Queen, was her
intermediary with her and through her to the King. The previous
petition to the King and letter to the Queen passed through her hands.
She wrote in return to Arbella:

This day her Majesty hath seen your ladyship's letter. Her Majesty says
that when she gave your petition to his Majesty, he did take it well
enough, but gave no other answer than that 'ye had eaten of the forbidden tree'. This was all her Majesty commanded me to say to your ladyship
to this purpose, but withall did remember her kindly to your ladyship, and
sent you this little token in witness to the continuance of her Majesty's
favour to your ladyship. Now where your ladyship desires me to deal
openly and freely with you, I protest I can say nothing on knowledge, for
I never spoke to any of that purpose but to the Queen; but the wisdom
of this state, with the example how some of your quality in the like case
has been used, makes me fear that ye shall not find so easy end to your
troubles as ye expect or I wish.[9]

Lady Drummond would have been as aware as Arbella as to how those who married against the royal will had suffered in the recent past. Arbella replied to this letter, enclosing a pair of gloves that she had embroidered for the Queen:

Good Cousin, I pray you present her Majesty my most humble thanks for the continuance of her Majesty's favour towards me that I received in your letter, which has so cheered me as I hope that I shall be the better to pass over my sorrow until it please God to move his Majesty's heart to compassion of me, whilst I may thereby assure myself I remain in her Majesty's favour, though all other worldly comforts be withdrawn from me: and will not cease to pray to the Almighty to reward her Majesty for her gracious regard of me in this distress with all happiness to her Royal self and hers. I pray you likewise present to her Majesty this piece of my work, which I humbly beseech her Majesty to accept in remembrance of the poor prisoner, her Majesty's most humble servant, that wrought them, in hope those royal hands will vouchsafe to wear them, which till I have the honour to kiss, I shall live in a great deal of sorrow. I take leave of you and rest Your very loving cousin Arbella Seymaure.[10]

She added another short note to this letter to Lady Drummond:

Good Cousin, I think myself as much beholden to you as if my man had brought me assurance of his Majesty's favours by her Majesty's means because I find your kindness in remembering me and preventing suspicions. But I cannot rest satisfied till I may know what disaster of mine hindreth his Majesty's goodness towards me, having such a mediatrix to plead so just and honest a cause as mine. Therefore I pray you with all earnestness let me know freely what hath been done concerning me, so wishing you all honour and happiness I take leave.

That Arbella thought the King's harsh treatment of her was out of character – and should not be compared to previous matrimonial disasters in the family – is obvious from this letter. She was, however, unaware of the King's poor state of health at the time he heard the news of her marriage. That he was very obstinate was a fact she chose to ignore.

The following letter was carried by a servant called Smith, who also

carried the only known extant letter from Arbella to William, although
we know that at this time they corresponded with each other regularly.
He was unwell, and she was very worried about his health, and she also
mentions her own. A bad cold and her face swollen with neuralgia often
heralded an attack of porphyria.

> Sir, I am extremely sorry to hear that you have not been well. I pray you
> let me know truly how you do, and what was the cause of it; for I am not
> satisfied with the reason Smith gives for it. But if it be a cold, I will impute
> it to some sympathy that exists between us, having myself gotten a
> swollen cheek at the same time with a cold. For God's sake, let not your
> grief of mind work on your body. You may see by me what inconveniences
> it may bring one to. And no fortune, I assure you, daunts me so much as
> the weakness of body I find in myself; for 'si nous vivons l'age d'un veau',
> as Marot says, we may by God's grace, be happier than we look for in
> being suffered to enjoy ourselves with his Majesty's favour. But if we be
> not able to live to it, I, for my part, shall think myself a pattern of misfor-
> tune in enjoying so great a blessing as you so little a while. No separation
> but that deprives me of the comfort of you, for wheresoever you be, or in
> what state soever you are, it sufficeth me you are mine. Rachel wept, and
> would not be comforted, because her children were no more; and that
> indeed is the remedyless sorrow, and none else. And therefore God bless
> us for that, and I will hope well of the rest, though I see no apparent hope.
> But I am sure God's book mentions many of his children in as great dis-
> tress that have done well after, even in this world. I assure you nothing
> the state can do with me can trouble me so much as the news of your
> being ill doth. And you see when I am troubled, I trouble you too with
> tedious kindness, for so I think you will account so long a letter, yourself
> not having written to me for this good while so much as how you do. But,
> sweet sir, I speak not this to trouble you with writing but when you please.
> Be well, and I shall account myself happy in being your faithful, loving
> wife, Arb. S.[11]

The old Earl of Hertford was appalled at the predicament his grandson was in, so similar to his own on his marriage to Catherine Grey.
Although he provided William with an allowance, he was much too
frightened of royal displeasure to plead for his grandson's release. In a
letter he wrote to Lord Salisbury on 2 October 1610 he makes no men-

tion of the problem but does mention that the King had been ill, and he congratulated him on his recovery. 'Your lordship could not have sent me any news so pleasing as to hear of his Majesty's health, which being lately crazed [ill], thanks be unto the Almighty for so perfect a recovery.'[12] If Hertford knew of the King's illness at this critical time for William and Arbella, they must have also been aware of it, which may be the reason that Arbella remained hopeful of his changing his mind once he had recovered.

William's brother Francis was a staunch ally, and Arbella in a letter to him thanks him for his sympathy. 'Howsoever higher powers cross the greater part of my happiness in depriving me for a time of your dear brother, my husband, I may not be altogether a stranger to your family, and yourself in particular, whose extraordinary kindness at this time shall be requited, God willing, with the redoubled love of so near alliance.' A letter from William to Francis also thanks him for his kindness while grumbling about his grandfather.[13]

For several months William and Arbella were left in peace. William did not petition the King himself, and Arbella's petitions went unanswered. Apart from their enforced separation they were probably happy enough away from court, and both lived in reasonable comfort once William's conditions in the Tower improved. However, the situation changed after January 1611 when news reached the King's ears that Sir Thomas Parry was being far too lenient with Arbella and that she had enjoyed assignations with her husband. This renewed the King's fear of a child resulting from the marriage.

The King, plainly recovered from his illness, was at Royston hunting, and not even Arbella's behaviour could distract him from that to attend to state business until March. Early in the month Arbella sent a petition to the Lord Chief Justice of England and the Lord Chief Justice of the Common Pleas.

My Lords – Whereas I have been long restrained from my liberty, which is as much to be regarded as my life, and am appointed, as I understand to be removed far from these Courts of Justice where I ought to be examined, tried and then condemned or cleared, to remote parts, whose courts I hold unfitted for the trial of my offence: this is to beseech your lordships to enquire by a Habeas Corpus or other usual form of law what is my fault; and if upon examination by your Lordships I shall therefore

be justly convicted, let me endure such punishments by your lordships'
sentence as is due to such an offender. And if your lordships may not or
will not of yourselves grant unto me the ordinary relief of a distressed
subject, then I beseech you to become humble intercessors to his Majesty
that I may receive such benefit of justice as both his Majesty by oath,
those of his blood not excepted, hath promised, and the laws of this realm
afford to all others. And though unfortunate woman (that I am) I should
obtain neither, yet I beseech your lordships retain me in your good opinion, and judge charitably until I be proved to have committed any
offence, either against God or His Majesty, deserving so long restraint or
separation from my lawful husband. So praying for your lordships, I
remain your afflicted poor suppliant, A.S.[13]

This petition, like the rest, went unanswered. On 4 March the Earl of
Rutland reported, 'That on Thursday last the Viscount Fenton was sent
to Lambeth to the Lady Arbella with directions to will her to prepare for
her journey to Durham which I think will be before the King's return.'
On 13 March the King issued a royal warrant from Royston to the
Bishop of Durham committing the 'Lady Arbella Seymour' to his
custody. Fenton was married to Arbella's cousin and childhood friend
Elizabeth Pierrepoint.

At the same time that the shattering news reached Arbella that she
was to be removed into the custody of the Bishop of Durham, making all
future contact with her husband impossible, she had a letter from her
old friend and retainer Mrs Alice Collingwood begging her for help. She
had not seen her husband, Francis Collingwood, for four years, after he
was imprisoned in the Tower as a recusant in 1604 on the charge of slan-
dering the King. She could not have known that Arbella was now in an
equally powerless position.[14]

On 13 March King James issued the warrant to the Bishop of
Durham.

James R. Right Reverend Father in God, and trusty and well beloved, –
we greet you well. Whereas our cousin the Lady Arbella hath highly
offended us in seeking to marry herself without our knowledge (to whom
she hath the honour to be near in blood), and in proceeding afterwards to
a full conclusion with the selfsame person (for many just causes) we had
forbidden her to marry; after he had in our presence, and before our

council, forsworn all interest as concerning her, either past or present, with solemn protestations upon his allegiance, in her hearing, never to renew any such motion again. For as much as it is more necessary for us to make some such demonstration of the just sense and feeling we have, after so great an indignity offered to us, as may make others know by her example that no respect of personal affection can make us neglect those considerations wherein both the honour and order of the state is interested, we have therefore thought good, out of trust in your fidelity and discretion, to remit to your care and custody the person of our said cousin, requiring and authorizing you hereby to carry her down in your company to any house of yours as unto you shall seem best and most convenient, there to remain in such sort as shall be set down to you by directions from the council, or any six of them to whom we have both declared our pleasure for the matter of her restraint, and have also given in charge, upon conference with you, to take order for all things necessary either for her health or otherwise. This being as you see, the difference between us and her – that whereas she hath abounded towards us in disobedience and ingratitude, we are (on the contrary) still apt to temper the severity of our justice with grace and favour towards her, as may well appear by the course we have taken to commit her only to your custody, to whose house she may be so well assured to receive all good usage, and see more fruit and exercise of religion and virtue than many other places. For all which this shall be your sufficient warrant. From Royston, this 13th March 1611.[15]

A warrant was also issued to Sir Thomas Parry ordering him to deliver Arbella to the Bishop of Durham.

After our very hearty commendations. Whereas it hath pleased his Majesty by letters under his royal signature to give orders to the right reverend father in God, the Bishop of Durham, to receive into his charge the person of the Lady Arbella Seymaure, to be carried down and conveyed from hence in his company to such house of his as shall seem best and most convenient, there to remain in such sort and according to such directions as are contained in the said letters. For as much as she was committed to your charge by His Majesty's commandment, and that it is meet the like order be taken for your discharge. These are therefore to will and require you, according to his Majesty's good pleasure in that behalf, to deliver the person of the said lady unto our very good lord, the Bishop of Durham, to be by him conveyed as aforesaid, which we require you to perform this present Friday. For which this shall be sufficient warrant. And we bid you heartily farewell. From Whitehall, the 15th day of March [1611].[16]

Among the signatories of both the warrants was Arbella's uncle, the Earl of Shrewsbury.

William James, the Bishop of Durham, was fifty-nine at the time, a rather frail man, and he found his task a formidable one. In happier circumstances Arbella would have rather enjoyed his company. He was an excellent scholar, having studied at Christ Church, Oxford. Later he became Master of University College, Oxford, and Vice-Chancellor of the university. He owned the magnificent Auckland Castle and was renowned as an excellent host. But from the moment the news reached Arbella that she was to be banished to Durham, with no hope of seeing her husband again, she became extremely distressed and, as had become the pattern, very ill. The long duration of her house captivity was wearing down her fragile constitution, and the severe cold, which she mentioned in her letter to William, may have triggered another attack of porphyria.

By the time she left Lambeth on 15 March she maintained that she was too ill to travel, but the Bishop and Dr Moundford, her doctor, managed to get her into a litter *en route* to Barnet, which was to be the first leg of the journey. After several hours of travel, stopping many times because of her sickness, the party arrived at Highgate at about ten o'clock at night, at which point Arbella refused to go any further. A warrant was issued to Sir William Bond, who owned a fine house on Highgate Hill, to provide her with accommodation for a night.

Forasmuch as here is some occasion to make provision for one night's lodging for the Lady Arbella, in respect that she cannot conveniently recover Barnet, some things being wanted for her journey this afternoon, contrary to our expectations, we have thought good to entreat you not to refuse such a courtesy as the lending of a couple of chambers for her ladyship; because we doubt the inns there are full of inconveniences. By doing whereof you shall give us cause to report well of you to His Majesty. And so we commit you to God.[17]

Sir William Bond's sister was married to Sir Richard Martin, the previous owner of the house. He was brother-in-law of Sir Julius Caesar, Chancellor of the Exchequer and later Master of the Rolls, who owned a large house at Highgate.

It was obvious to Arbella's physician that her illness was not imaginary and that she was quite unfit to travel. The house where she stayed, now known as Lauderdale House, still stands on the edge of Waterlow Park in Highgate.[18] Permission was granted that she could remain in Highgate for a few days; in fact she was to stay for a week. A document exists in the Talbot MSS at Longleat which shows that during this time she and William signed a document, an original discharge of accounts given by Seymour and Arbella to Hugh Crompton, which strongly suggests that William managed to see Arbella at Highgate. It was signed on the day she left for Barnet; Rodney and Kirton are the witnesses. These financial arrangements seem to have been made with a future escape in mind.

Still very unwell, she was forced to move a further six miles north to Barnet on 21 March, but she was so ill that she nearly died. The old Bishop was so appalled by her condition and his task of attending to her that he handed over her supervision to Sir James Croft – a friend of Arbella's whom she had visited on her progress – on the grounds of his own ill health and also that he had to report to the King at Royston and go to prepare his palace for her in Durham once he had seen her settled in a suitable house.

ESCAPE

Gilbert Shrewsbury, who was unwell himself at this time, wrote to Dr Moundford at Barnet thanking him for his care of Arbella on the arduous journey. The Earl told the King of her being forced out of her bed to travel in a litter when she was so ill. James, still believing that his cousin was not so much physically ill as merely making a fuss, replied, 'It was enough to make any sound man sick to be carried in a bed in that manner. It is much more for her whose impatient and unquiet spirits heapeth upon herself for greater indisposition of body.' Shrewsbury asked Moundford to write to his wife Mary and tell her about the situation at Barnet. It was probably this letter that inspired her aunt to make plans for Arbella's escape.

James, in spite of his own illness, was determined to have a full report on Arbella's state of health from the the physician who cared for his sons, the highly esteemed Dr Hammond. On 26 March he sent him to the inn at Barnet where she was temporarily housed, convinced that the report would say she was quite fit enough to travel. The physician spent three days with her and reported back to the Council on 28 March, Gilbert Shrewsbury was present at this meeting and reported back to Dr Moundford on the following day. James was not pleased with his findings. She was obviously a very sick woman. Among her many symptoms was the abnormal state of her urine, which was very dark and congested. Shrewsbury's letter read as follows:

I heartily thank you (good Mr Doctor) for your letter by Mr Smith, and I am still very sorry that you cannot give us of the good estate of her ladyship's body than we can read in your said letter. I was present yesterday morning when Mr Dr Hammond made report to the lords in what state he found my Lady Arbella, being this in substance, that she is assuredly very weak, her pulse dull and melancholy for the most part, yet sometimes uncertain; her water bad, showing very great obstructions; her countenance very heavy, pale and wan; nevertheless she was free (he said) from any fever, or any actual sickness, but of his conscience he protested that she was in no case to travel until God restored her to some better strength both of body and mind. (Somewhat more he reported of the speeches that passed between her Ladyship and him, though briefly though very pertinent and in very discreet and friendly manner.) He attendeth on the Princes (as always he doth) to Royston on Monday next, and then he is himself to relate to his Majesty, as he did to us; for at that time his Majesty was so extremely pestered with dispatches upon his going away, as there could be no full report unto him of any particulars, only he was told of her weakness. All her Ladyship's friends in general are glad of the Bishop's departing, and her stay for a time where she is to be, verily that she will likewise receive great comfort therein; and how far soever her own melancholy thoughts (which have gotten the upper hand of her) have prevailed to lay nothing but despair before her eyes, yet the greatest, nearest and wisest about his Majesty that I do speak with doth persuade themselves that her imprisonment (wheresoever it be) and His Majesty's disfavour to her is not like to continue long; and therefore I am bound to believe them, or else I must conceive they have neither honour or conscience, for such is their protestations to me. God grant that her Ladyship may be of the same mind, and then I should not much doubt of her speedy recovery, which heartily praying for, I will here take my hearty leave of you and remain Your assured loving friend, Gilbert Shrewsbury. At Brod Street this 29th of March, 1611. To my very good friend Dr Moundford.[1]

Shrewsbury had received a letter from Dr Moundford the day before expressing doubt about the efficacy of the cordials Dr Hammond had prescribed for Arbella's deep depression. She had met Dr Hammond before, so was willing to comply with any treatment he administered. 'I am sure', he wrote, 'that neither of these prescribed can warrant either amendment of her grief or continuance of life, if some contentment of mind is not joined with physic, which I, with all due respect, will cause to be administered when time and opportunity of place shall be afforded us. In the mean time I am forced to instil in cordials, though with some fear of the consequences in the lady's weak, excitable state, preferring to cherish her to live, rather than by waiting all circumstances incident to the perfect recovery of such an imperfect body, do nothing.'

Arbella meanwhile was well enough to send a petition to the Privy Council.

I protest I am in so weak case as I verily think it would be the cause of my death to be removed any whither at this time, though it were to a place of my liking. My late discomfortable journey, from which I have not yet recovered, had almost ended my days, and I have never since gone out of a very few little and hot rooms, and am in many ways unfit to take the air. I trust your lordships will not look I should be so un-Christian as to be the cause of my own death, and I leave it to your lordships' wisdom to consider what the world would conceive if I should be violently forced to do it. Therefore I beseech your lordships to be suitors on my behalf, that I may have some time given me to recover my strength, which should the sooner do if I was not continually molested. And I will hope and pray that God will incline His Majesty's heart every way to more compassion towards me, who rest very humbly at your lordships' command. A.S.[2]

Arrangements were made for Arbella to stay at a house belonging to a well-known resident of East Barnet, Mr Thomas Conyers, at Church Hill House, which stood on a hill very near the church. He had only recently acquired it, and when she arrived it was not ready for her occupation.[3] He was paid twenty shillings a week for it by them, and he was not living there himself. Meanwhile temporary accommodation was found for the party at an inn. It is probable that the accommodation at the house was found with the assistance of Sir William Bond, whose estate was adjacent to that of Sir Jasper Cholmeley. Sir Jasper was a relative of the Conyers family through the marriage of his third son William to Katherine Pym, who was Thomas Conyers's niece, and William also lived in East Barnet.

Sir James Croft, who with his cousin Sergeant Minors had taken responsibility for Arbella, was an acquaintance of hers whose footman had accompanied her on her progress from Toddington to Northampton in 1609. He now wrote to Salisbury on 31 March that Arbella had tried to dress herself as well as her extreme weakness would allow for her move from their temporary accommodation in Barnet to Conyers's house, but that it was delayed as the house in East Barnet was still not ready. The effect of this delay was to provoke a violent attack of hysteria and weeping on the part of Arbella.[4] The following day her companions finally moved her the short distance to Church Hill House, but she was extremely ill during the journey.

On 25 March James granted her a month's respite from the continuation of her journey to Durham, which was an enormous relief to Arbella, and she gradually improved. The Bishop, having seen her safely installed in East Barnet, started on his journey back to Durham, stopping on his way at Royston to report to the King. He wrote to Dr Moundford and Sir James Croft from Trinity College, Cambridge, on 17 April.

My Worshipful and very worthy friends, The first day of my departure from you a very vehement fit of a tertian fever took me in Enfield Chase, so as with much ado I got that night to Hertford, where I had, I thank God, a very sick night; a second fit took me the 3rd of this instant, between Royston and Caxton, at an ale house where I stayed (but rested little) almost two days and a night; whence I came hither the 4th, where I have stayed now twelve days, and have had six very sharp fits, notwithstanding Mr Butler and other physicians here have taken much blood of me, whereby I am become weak. Yet they put me in hope that the worst is past; and as soon as it shall please God that my fits shall leave me, I will go on though it be *lento pede*.

I attended his Majesty at Royston, who was certified, as soon as I lighted from my horse, of my coming hither, and required my presence in the morning. I was no sooner come into the court, but I was presently brought to his Majesty, who asked me of the Lady Arbella, and where I left her. I told his Majesty of her estate in her three removes; of the grief which she conceived at his Majesty's indignation; of her hearty and zealous prayers for him and his; of her willingness, if it might so please him, even to sweep his chamber. Whereunto it pleased his Majesty to call the Prince, who was then in the same room. I do not see but that his Majesty is well pleased with the time she hath to recover strength, and that he had an especial care that she should be used and respected as a noble lady of her birth and nearness to him; and time may work that which in this shortness cannot be effected. I pray you present my duty and service unto her, to pray her to remember what I oftentimes, out of a true heart (as yourselves in my hearing have done) have said unto her. So shall she best please God by her obedience, satisfy his Majesty, comfort her own conscience, enable her good friends to speak for her, and stop the mouths (if any there be) who envy her restitution into his Majesty's favour. My poor opinion is that if she wrong not her self, God in time will move his Majesty's heart to have compassion upon her. I signified unto his Majesty, both your cares and pains in this his service, as also honest Serjeant Minors' pains and care, which his Majesty seemed well to believe and much to approve.

Your time now almost expireth, and I am but thus far on my way; and I pray God the noble lady and me may in good time meet in the North, which we shall the better do, if in all these things she submit herself unto the will of her God and her Sovereign.[5]

It appears that those who were close to the King felt that he would relent in the end and restore her to his favour at Court, but he insisted on her being banished to Durham. Prince Henry was still most anxious for her welfare, and the fact that James included him in the interviews with her custodians should have given Arbella hope. However, she was not prepared to be patient.

She used her respite in Barnet to plan an escape to France with William, aided by her Aunt Mary and close friends. The same day that the Bishop wrote to Dr Moundford, Sir James Croft wrote to the Privy Council, reporting on Arbella's progress.

She is somewhat better and lightsome than heretofore, but that not otherwise than that she hath not walked as yet the length of her bed-chamber, to my knowledge; neither do I find her at any time otherwise than in her naked bed, or in her clothes upon the bed. Concerning her ladyship's mind, it is so much dejected, as she apprehendeth nothing but fear and danger in their ugliest forms, conceiting always the worst, and much worse than any way can happen unto her of danger. As for her going this journey, or that his Majesty should dispose of her at his pleasure, she doth not gainsay, but the horrors of her utter ruin and end which hourly present themselves to her fantasy, occasioned (as she discovereth herself unto me) by the remoteness of the place whereunto she must go, driveth her to utter despair, or to be able to live out one only year; where otherwise, if she were left, as her ladyship saith, in some convenient place, not so clean out of the world as she termeth Durham to be, she would gather to herself some weak hopes of more gentle fortune in time to come. These and the like are the best and pleasingest discourses that at any time I can have with her ladyship, whereunto whatsoever I can reply to the contrary giveth her no manner of satisfaction at all.[6]

Ten days after his letter to the Privy Council Croft was still very worried about Arbella's health and knew she was quite unfit to travel. The month's sojourn at Barnet would be up at the end of April, so on the 27th he sent Sergeant Minors to London to plead for an extension to her stay there. Minors's reply to him was unsatisfactory.

I told of my lady's weak estate, and afterwards they told me the king's absolute resolution, which is directly for Durham, for which she must prepare, although the journey be never so little, to go on Monday next which was the longest day I could get. I pray you let her know that some of the greatest of them did in solemn oaths protest that they find, by his Majesty's resolution, that there shall be no long abode for her there, but his Majesty intended her good in short time after, but that his Majesty kept that in his breast till he saw conformity; but if his Majesty be King, he says he will not alter this resolution. Therefore I pray you use your best means to prepare her ladyship for the journey at that day; for there is no doubt it will follow for her honour's good.[7]

In spite of these further assurances that her stay in Durham would only be a short one, she still protested that she was quite unfit for such a journey, and apparently Dr Moundford and Sir James Croft agreed with her. The day for her intended departure passed, and they decided to plead for an extension of her stay to the King, now returned from Royston, and the Council. The interview took place in early May. Meanwhile Arbella, who was recovered sufficiently to write, sent a letter to the King. It was well worded and did much to persuade him to give her more time to recuperate before the long journey.

'May it please your excellent Majesty,' she wrote:

Though it hath pleased God to lay so many crosses upon me as I account myself the most miserable creature living, yet none is so grievous to me as the loss of your Majesty's favour, which appeareth, not so much to my unspeakable grief in any other effect of it (though the least of many it hath already brought forth is sufficient for my utter ruin) as in that your Majesty giveth credence (as I heard) to those sinister reports which impute that to my obstinacy which proceedeth merely out of necessity; not willing that I might be thought guilty of hastening my own death by any voluntary action of mine, having first endeavoured, by all good means, to make my extreme weakness known to your Majesty by my Lord Fenton, and by the lords of your Majesty's most honourable Privy Council by writing, and many other ways before my remove. But my misfortune being such as not only any protestation of mine own, but the reiterated testimony of such grave persons as advertised the like, seemed of less weight than the traducements of some whisperers. But nothing availing me, certainly I had suddenly perished if your Majesty had not speedily had compassion on me in granting me this time of stay for my recovery; to which if it may please your Majesty of your gracious goodness to add three weeks more, Dr Moundford hopes I may recover so much strength as may enable me to travel. And I shall ever be willing, whilst I breathe, to yield your Majesty most humble and dutiful obedience as to my sovereign, for whose felicity for ever in all things I cease not to pray, and in all fortunes rest Your Majesty's most humble and faithful subject, A.S.[8]

This letter has another paper attached to it written in another hand, probably dictated by Arbella and signed 'J', where she promises, as a proof of her obedience, 'to undergo the journey after this time expires without any resistance or refusal, to do such things as are fit for me to do to make my journey the less painful or perilous; being now assured that your Majesty hath no purpose to make my correction my ruin in any sort, as I will hope confidently when I have herein satisfied the duty'. Arbella was well aware that the King was determined that his pride should be satisfied by her promise to obey him when she was fit enough to travel. A marginal note to this letter states that 'the obedience without the journey is enough if the King desire but his honour saved'.

Dr Moundford sent a report on his appearance before the King and Council to the Bishop of Durham.

James, in the hearing of the Prince and the Lords of his Majesty's Council, did yield that one other month should be employed in her perfect cure, which new month began on the 11th day of this present May. During our attendance on his Majesty he used not one unkind or wrathful word of her, but mildly taxed her obstinacy, the conceit whereof I find did spring from such accidents as befell upon our first removes, reported to him very untruly, with terms of violence offered by my lady to such as were used in that service. His Majesty's resolution was that to Durham she should come, if he were King. We answered that we made no doubt of her obedience. He said 'Obedience is that required; which being performed, I will do more for her than she expecteth.' The premier reason which moved his Majesty to the grant of this second month was her submission in a letter to his Highness, with all due acknowledgement of her recovery from the grave by time most graciously granted her by him. This letter was penned by her in the best of terms (as she can do right well) and accompanied with matter best fitting His Highness and her. It was often read without offence, nay I may truly say, even commended by himself with the applause of the Prince and Council.[9]

Once more the Prince seems to be on her side and anxious for her welfare in spite of her marriage.

Arbella had a great capacity for inspiring affection and loyalty, not only from her servants but from everyone she met. Lady Chandos, widow of the third Baron Chandos, was one of the friends who tried to help her during her stay in Barnet. She appears to have been staying with her daughter, Lady Kennedy, who as the beautiful Elizabeth Brydges had attracted the attention of Essex and the jealousy of Queen Elizabeth.

Lady Chandos wrote to Dr Moundford on Good Friday 1611, offering to help with the care of Arbella in her sickness with any cordial she might fancy.

Doctor Moundford, – I desire the widow's prayer, with my humble service, may by you be presented to the Lady Arbella, who I hope God will so fortify her mind, as she will take this cross with such patience as may be to His pleasing, who, as this day signifies, took upon Him a good deal more for us; and when he seeth time He will send comfort to the afflicted. I pray you if you want for the honourable lady what is in this house, you will send for it; for most willingly the master and mistress of the house would have her ladyship command it. If the drink do like my lady, spare not to send. The knight and my daughter remember their kind commendations to yourself. So I commit you to God, and rest as your friend Francis Chandos. To my friend Dr Moundford at Barnet.[10]

The extra time gave Arbella a chance to regain some of her strength. She was still very weak and exhausted, but from the accounts of her expenses at this time it appears that a coach and horses were hired for her from a Thomas Webster for the not inconsiderable sum of £73 6s. She was obviously granted a certain amount of freedom to drive round the countryside in the coach when she felt well enough, perhaps visiting friends such as Lady Chandos. These trips would have improved her health and spirits and made her feel less under house arrest.

Her Aunt Mary made one final effort to obtain a pardon for her niece through the King's favourite, Lord Rochester. But he refused to have anything to do with it, being a friend of Lord Northampton, a staunch Roman Catholic, always strongly opposed to Arbella's claim to the throne.

Mary was a difficult but clever and determined woman, much like her mother Bess, and she expended an enormous amount of energy, time and money in planning William's and Arbella's escape across the Channel. She must have been in constant contact with them both, although no letters between them survive. Arbella's steward Hugh Crompton was in the plot, also Arbella's maid, Mrs Bradshaw, who had witnessed the wedding, and of course Edward Rodney who was helping William. A large amount of money was required for the operation, for bribes, the fare to France, transport and accommodation. Arbella managed to raise £2,800, an enormous sum, £1,400 of which came from her aunt. Not to arouse suspicion, Mary said the money was given to Arbella for a piece of needlework undertaken by Mary Queen of Scots in Arbella's possession, which she priced at £850; the balance was to be used to pay off Arbella's debts before her departure for Durham.

The summer of 1611 was extremely hot. We hear of the exceptional weather in the notes of James's physician, Dr Mayerne, who had arrived in England that year. Mayerne reports that the heat was so overwhelming that James's face developed a vesicular rash, accompanied by violent headaches, vomiting and acute pain.[11]

It was unfortunate for Arbella that, as she was gradually recovering from her attack James was getting worse, both mentally and physically, and was now in no mood to forgive her.

Mary Shrewsbury had obviously been a frequent visitor at East Barnet, but the plan of escape that she masterminded had two flaws. To begin with, too many people were involved, and, second, no contingency plan was drawn up if Arbella, William and their attendants failed to make the prearranged rendezvous.

The scheme was fairly simple. Arbella's two most devoted servants, Hugh Crompton and Anne Bradshaw, who were to go to France with her, were replaced in the East Barnet household by the parson's wife, Mrs Adam, and William Markham, whose family lived near Rufford and was well known to Arbella. Arbella, who had been allowed a certain amount of freedom once she started to recover, was to tell Mrs Adam that she wished to leave the house for a night to say farewell to her husband before the departure for Durham, scheduled for 5 June. Crompton was to bring her a man's disguise to wear, and he was also to take horses to an inn about a mile away for Arbella and himself. Markham was to accompany Arbella on the walk from the house to the inn. They would ride to London, a distance of about fourteen miles, hoping to arrive at the river inn at Blackwall at around six o'clock, where William, who should have escaped from the Tower by then, would meet them with his friend Edward Rodney. The baggage was to be collected the day before by Rodney who would hire a room at St Mary Overy opposite the Tower to store it and later take it to the inn at Blackwall. A boat would row them down to Leigh, where a French vessel was to meet them to take them across the Channel.

Sir John More described what actually happened to his master, the diplomat Sir Ralph Winwood, former Ambassador in Paris and later Secretary of State, who was in The Hague at the time.

On Monday last, in the afternoon, my Lady Arbella, lying at Mr Conyers's house, near Highgate, having induced her keepers and attendants into security by the fair show of conformity and willingness to go on her journey towards Durham, which the next day she must have done, and in the meantime disguising herself, by drawing a pair of great French-fashioned hose over her petticoats, pulling on a man's doublet, a man-like peruke, with long locks over her hair, a black hat, a black cloak, russet boots with red tops, and a rapier by her side, walked forth, between three and four of the clock with Markham. After they had gone a mile and a half to a sorry inn, where Crompton attended with horses, she grew very sick and faint, so as the ostler who held the stirrups said that gentleman would hardly hold out to London; yet, being set on a good gelding astride, in an unwonted fashion, the stirring of the horse brought blood enough to her face; and so she rode on towards Blackwall, where arriving about six of the clock, finding there in readyness two men, a gentlewoman and a chambermaid, with one boat full of Mr Seymour's and her trunks, and another boat for their persons, they hastened from thence towards Woolwich.[12]

He does not mention that, to Arbella's horror, William and Rodney were not there as arranged. After waiting nearly two hours Arbella was persuaded by her attendants that she must continue her journey downriver before the tide changed. Very reluctantly, having removed the wig, she wrapped herself in a cloak and hood, got into one of the two boats with Mrs Bradshaw and was rowed towards Leigh. William's plans for escape from the Tower had been simple; no doubt he had left it in a similar fashion many times. Instructing his barber, Thomas Batten, to tell any visitors that he had gone to bed for the night with toothache, he disguised himself as a carter's labourer. Billets, or firewood, were delivered to his lodging regularly by the carter, and William planned to walk out of the Tower behind him when he had delivered the logs. He had obviously intended to leave in good time to meet Rodney at the Iron Gate and walk down to Blackwall to liaise with Arbella. But, by some misfortune, the carter must have arrived very late, and William did not leave the Tower until eight o'clock, by which time Arbella was already on her way downriver to Leigh.

Even then all could have been well if the parties concerned had decided beforehand that if they missed each other at Blackwall they should proceed separately to catch the French boat or any other ship that would take them, meeting up later in France.

Two boats left Blackwall, one with Arbella and Mrs Bradshaw and the other with Markham, Crompton, Edward Reeves and the luggage. They rowed slowly downriver hoping that William would overtake them. By the time they reached Woolwich there was still no sign of him, and at Greenwich the boatmen refused to go any further because it was now dark. They were eventually persuaded to continue the journey after being offered double the fare. When they reached Tilbury the boatmen insisted on going ashore for refreshment, and the vessels finally reached Leigh in the early dawn. The French ship was anchored eight miles away, out of sight, so they hailed the first ship they saw, bound for Berwick, and offered the master, John Bright, a large bribe to take them to Calais. He refused but pointed out the French ship, which was now in sight about a mile and a half away. The undue pressure that had been put on him to change course aroused his suspicions, and when he was later cross-examined in the aftermath of the incident he was able to give a very accurate description of the group on board.[13] When at last they boarded the French boat, Arbella was still loath to leave without William but was finally persuaded to proceed to France alone. But as they had missed the tide they had to wait two hours before they could set sail.

Arbella and William had appreciated the support and friendship they had received from his younger brother Francis after they were married. He was twenty-one at the time of the escape, much in awe of his grandfather and, like the rest of his family, in perpetual fear of arousing the anger of the King. Rodney, before he left England, had perhaps unwisely written to Francis hinting vaguely that he would not be returning for some time. The note was to be delivered at eight o'clock on the Tuesday morning, by which time Rodney assumed that they would all be safely in France. Francis, on receiving the letter, was immediately anxious for his brother and rushed off to the Tower, where he forced the barber to open William's room and to his horror found it empty. Francis described what happened in a letter to his grandfather, the Earl of Hertford.

4th of June, 1611. My most honourable and dear Lord and Grandfather, Lately (I may say unfortunately) my brother escaped out of the Tower. Edward Rodney left a letter behind him to be delivered to me which letter I received upon Tuesday following at eight o'clock. The contents of it was this: He desired me to excuse him in he did not acquaint me with his unfortunate business (as I may well term it) besides that they had decided to tell it to none, by which means they might the better keep it from your Lordship, knowing your Lordship would presently have acquainted the King therewith. This was the main scope of his letter which I had no sooner received but I presently mistrusted that which in less than half an hour after I had found to be most true, which was that my brother was gone. My self being come to his lodging, I asked his man for him, who told me that he had not slept of all that night, and that he would not that morning be troubled. I was not therewith satisfied, telling him that I must and would see him, which when he perceived he could not resist, he confessed the truth, which he had no sooner done, but at the very same instant comes the Lieutenant, to whom I showed this letter of Edmund Rodney, which I had intended presently to show the the Lord Treasurer. The Lieutenant being acquainted herewith went straight to Greenwich.[14]

It would appear that up to this time no alarm had been given from Church Hill House that Arbella was missing. The loyalty and affection that Sir James Croft and the rest of the household had for her – as well as a few bribes – may have kept them silent. She had probably been absent from the house before, and they were still expecting her to return in time to prepare for the journey to Durham.

It was the discovery that William had escaped from the Tower that alerted the King to her flight. His anger on hearing the news was out of all proportion to the offence. Lord Nottingham, the Lord High Admiral, tried to calm the King down, and a correspondent of the diplomat Sir Ralph Winwood wrote, 'James's reaction was in great excess of the importance of the reality of the escape. The danger was not likely to have been very great in regard that their pretensions are so many degrees removed [by the direct claim of James's two sons], and they ungraceful [out of favour] both in their person and their houses. So as a hot alarm taken of the matter will make them more illustrious in the world's eye than they are, or being let alone, ever would have been. The escape is said to fill his Majesty with fearful imaginations, and the Prince, who cannot be removed from any settled opinion.'[15]

No doubt the shock of hearing the news of Arbella's escape would have aggravated James's symptoms. The affair was a terrible blow to his pride and his belief in the divine right of kings. It was said that he had behaved as if it were as significant as the Gunpowder Plot, when in fact there was no danger to his throne or his life, as it was well known that William and Arbella had no desire to usurp him.

A proclamation was immediately issued:

Whereas we are given to understand that the Lady Arbella and William Seymour, second son to the Lord Beauchamp, being for divers great and heinous offences committed, the one to the Tower of London, and the other to a special guard, have found the means, by the wicked practices of divers lewd persons, as namely Markham, Crompton, Rodney and others, to break prison and make escape, on Monday the third day of

June, with an intent to transport themselves to foreign parts. We do hereby straitly charge and command all persons whatsoever, upon their allegiance and duty, not only to forbear to receive, harbour or assist them in their passage in any way, as they will answer it at their perils; but, upon the like charge and pain to use the best means they can for their apprehension and keeping them in safe custody, which we will take as an acceptable service. Given at Greenwich the 4th day of June, 1611 (*per Ipsum Regem*).[16]

When William and Rodney arrived at Leigh on the Tuesday morning the French boat was nowhere to be seen, so, hiring a small fishing boat for twenty shillings, they were rowed out to a collier, *Charles*, which was bound for Newcastle upon Tyne. But Rodney persuaded the master to take them to Calais for the handsome sum of £40. When examined by the Bailiff of Ipswich later, the master – who gave evidence to the Earl of Suffolk – described the party as consisting of one gentleman wearing a suit of red satin with silver and gold lace (Rodney), another young man in a 'suit of murray-coloured stuff', the third a Frenchman and the fourth a servant, William, who could have still been in his disguise as a labourer. Rodney did the negotiating. As they proceeded downriver at about noon, they spotted a French ship. They anchored at a buoy, and the French ship anchored about a mile and a half from them. Rodney told the master that this boat might be the one in which they had intended to get to France and asked him to row over to enquire. Instead of William going with the Frenchman they had with them, the master went with the Frenchman, who entered a cabin with one of the passengers. There the master saw a woman dressed in a waistcoat and petticoat sitting on the hatches. It is quite likely that she was either Arbella or Mrs Bradshaw, but as Arbella's group would not have given their names for fear of capture, and none of the party from the *Charles* would have recognized them, the master returned to the collier saying it was the wrong boat. It is of course possible that, fearing to lose such an excellent fare, the master decided to keep quiet to Rodney about the woman he saw on board and carry his wealthy passenger himself. The truth of the matter will never be known. Obviously William and Rodney were sufficiently satisfied to proceed with their journey on the *Charles*.

The wind remained against them for Calais, so they decided to make for Harwich where they stayed the night. The French ship was still anchored in the same place when they left for Harwich. The next day, the wind still being against them, they decided to make for Ostend, where they arrived a mile away from the town at eight o'clock on the Friday morning. They had told the master that they were leaving England because of a quarrel and duly paid him the £40, after which he returned to England.[17]

PRISONER IN THE TOWER

Lord Nottingham, the Lord High Admiral, was a perceptive man. He was sorry that Arbella and William had attempted to escape but told James, 'England will find no loss by their escape. The best that I do think as it falleth out, is that it do not agree to the world that there is any account made of them. The wind is bad and they cannot have gone far.'[1]

We know that William had already reached Ostend safely by the time Arbella was finally returned to England. She has been criticized by some historians for her hesitation in leaving England and lingering outside Calais instead of heading for safety. But, as far as her party was concerned, the obvious explanation for William not being at their rendezvous at the Blackwall inn and not catching up with them later would have been that either he had been unable to escape from the Tower or that he had escaped but been captured soon afterwards. Arbella would have been appalled at the idea of going to France without him, and the lesser of two evils would have been to stay in England to be as near him as possible. Her hesitation was understandable but fatal.

As soon as the news of her escape reached the King, Lord Nottingham instructed his admiral, Sir William Monson, to give chase. It seems likely that John Bright, the master of the brig that refused to take them to Calais, had betrayed them. In later years Monson ascribed much of his unpopularity with the English public to the fact that he had captured Arbella and bought her back to England, which suggests that her capture and imprisonment in the Tower were disapproved of by many.

Among the boats he sent out was a fast pinnacle, the *Adventure*, which caught up with the French boat and, after firing shots at her, forced her to surrender. Griffin Cockett, the *Adventure*'s captain, wrote the following dispatch to the Lord High Admiral on 5 June.

Right Honourable, After I had received direction from my Admiral for the intercepting of the Lady Arbella and Mr. William Seymour, we stood off, and under the South Sandhead we saw a small sail, which we chased, and proving little wind, we sent our boat with shot and pikes, and half the channel over our boat did overtake them, and making some few shot, they yielded, where we found divers passengers, among the rest, my Lady Arbella, her three men and one gentlewoman. We cannot find yet that Mr. Seymour is here. My lady saith that she saw him not, but hopeth that he got over. My lady came into the French barque at Quinborough, and is now aboard the *Adventure* safe until we shall receive further directions from your lordship. We do keep the barque with all those passengers in her until such time as we shall hear further from your Lordship. I humbly rest your Lordships humbly to command, Griffin Cockett. From aboard the *Adventure* off His Majesty's Downs, 5th June, 1611. For His Majesty's especial service to the Right Honourable the Lord High Admiral of England, my very good Lord and Master, Haste, haste, haste, post haste, haste post haste for your life. Downs 5th June o'clock afternoon 8.[2]

Monson, who had boarded the *Adventure* himself on its arrival at Sheppey, wrote straight away to Lord Salisbury asking what he should do with Arbella. He was frustrated by the slowness of the mail.

Right Honourable . . . Hearing the *Adventure* was so quickly returned to the Downs gave me the assurance she had met with the Lady Arbella, which made me hasten thither with all speed; and though as I said before, the master hath acquainted my Lord Admiral therewith, yet I thought it my duty not to direct my letter to any but your Lordship, and expect His Majesty's directions how to dispose of my Lady, for that I am unwilling that she should go ashore until I have further authority, but in the mean time she shall not want anything the shore can afford, or any other honourable usage . . . Your Lordship's in all service to be commanded, William Monson. For his Majesty's special service, to the Right Honourable my especially good Lord, the Earl of Salisbury, Lord High Treasurer of England. Haste, haste, haste, post haste for life, life. Aboard the Adventure the 6th, past 11 o'clock forenoon.[3]

The Earl of Hertford immediately wrote to Lord Salisbury on receiving Francis Seymour's alarming letter about his brother's escape. Hertford was summoned to court, but James must have been convinced that neither he nor any of his family took part in the escape. Hertford made no attempt to mediate on William's behalf and three weeks later wrote him a very stern letter, which was shown to Salisbury for his approval before it was sent.

The passengers on the French boat must have been very angry at being returned to England, where the captain, Tassin Corvé, was taken prisoner. Anyone who had anything to do with Arbella's and William's attempted escape was rounded up on 4 and 5 June, from the humble watermen to Dr Moundford and Sir James Croft. The Countess of Shrewsbury was committed to the Tower and Sir James Croft to the Fleet Prison. Dr Moundford was a close prisoner in the Gatehouse with Mrs Adams, the minister's wife from East Barnet. The total list of those committed to prison pending investigation into the escape conspiracy was as follows: Arbella and her aunt Mary Shrewsbury in the Tower; Hugh Crompton in the Fleet; William Markham in the Fleet; William's barber Batten and his butler in a dungeon in the Tower; Sir James Croft and Dr Moundford in the Fleet (but later removed); Mrs Adams and Edward Kirton in the Gatehouse; Tassin Corvé, the French skipper, and John Baisley, a waterman, in Newgate.[4]

On her arrival at the Tower Arbella was put in the same rooms in the Lieutenant's Lodgings that had been occupied by her grandmother Margaret Lennox on the marriage of her elder son Lord Darnley to Mary Queen of Scots. Mary Shrewsbury was also placed in the Lieu-tenant's Lodgings, and they appeared together before the Privy Council, in order to keep the investigation as private as possible. Arbella behaved impeccably, which meant that although she was weak and exhausted her mind was clear. Her aunt, on the other hand, was furious at not having a public hearing and said so in no uncertain terms. Sir John More described the scene to Winwood.

On Saturday last, the Countess of Shrewsbury was lodged in the Tower, where she is likely long to rest as well as the Lady Arbella. The last named lady answered the lords at her examination with good judgement and dis-cretion; but the other is said to be utterly without reason, crying out that all is but tricks and giggs; that she will answer nothing in private, and if she have offended the law will answer in public. She is said to have amassed a great sum of money to some ill use, £20,000 are known to be in her cash; and that she had made provision for more Bills of Exchange to her niece's use than she had knowledge of. And though the Lady Arbella hath not yet been found to incline to popery, yet her aunt made account belike that beyond the seas in the hands of Jesuits and Priests, either the stroke of their arguments or the pinch of poverty might force her to the other side.[5]

Mary had some of the best accommodation in the Tower, but she bitterly complained to her husband of the condition of her rooms. Although those who knew Mary well found her too much like her redoubtable mother Bess of Hardwick for comfort, her love and loyalty and generosity to Arbella, of whom she was very fond, were beyond doubt, and she had to suffer a lengthy imprisonment in consequence.

She was to remain in the Tower for two years, with one short break to nurse her husband. Crompton and Markham were tortured for little reason, as their part in the escape was well known. By November 1613 they were both released. As for poor Sir James Croft and Dr Moundford, who took no part in the conspiracy, they were released soon after Arbella had appeared before the Council. James, who was ill most of that summer and mentally unstable, showed no signs of relaxing the severity with which he was treating Arbella.[6]

In spite of this, during her first days in the Tower she did not give up hope of him forgiving her and asked to have her servants about her, particularly Lady Chaworth, whose husband had been her messenger in the Hardwick days. Her money and jewels were taken away from her and put in charge of Sir William Bowyer, who had instructions to sell what was necessary to pay for the cost of her capture. Her old friend Sir Christopher Yelverton tried to protect her interests. Strangely, James did not stop her allowance but carried on paying it right up to her death.

Few letters from her survive from this period. One that she wrote in these early days was to her cousin, Viscount Fenton, who was married to Elizabeth Pierrepoint. From this it is apparent that she had been very ill again since her arrival at the Tower, aggravated by the blow that she was not to be allowed to have her own servants to look after her and, moreover, was to be deprived of the necessities that she felt she required to cope with her illness.

My Lord, – The long acquaintance between us, and the good experience of your honourable dealing heretofore makes me not only hope but be most assured that if you knew my most discomfortable and distressed state, you would acquaint his Majesty withal and consequently procure my relief and redress as you have done other times. I have been sick even to the death, from which it hath pleased God miraculously to deliver me for this present danger, but find myself so weak by reason I have wanted those ordinary helps whereby most others in my case, be they never so poor or unfortunate soever, are preserved alive at least for charity; that unless I may be suffered to have those about me that I can trust, this sentence my Lord Treasurer after his Majesty's refusing that trifle of my work, by your persuasion, as I take it, will prove the certain and apparent cause of my death. Whereof I then thought good to advertise you that you both may the better be prepared in case you or either of you have possessed the King with such opinions of me, as thereupon I shall be suspected and restrained till help come too late, and be assured that neither physician nor other but whom I think good shall come about me whilst I live till I have His Majesty's favour, without which I desire not to live. And if you remember of old I dare to die so I be not guilty of my own death, and oppress others with my ruin too, if there be no other way, as God forbid, to whom I commit you, and rest assuredly as heretofore, if you be the same to me, your lordship's faithful friend, A.S. I can neither get clothes, nor posset ale, for example, or anything but ordinary diet, nor compliment fit for a sick body in my case when I call for it, not so much as a glister, saving your reverence.[7]

She obviously had grave misgivings about Fenton's and his wife's loyalty to her and suggested that he had encouraged the King to return a small present she had embroidered for him.

On arriving in Belgium William and Rodney made their way to the court of the Archduke in Bruges, where they received a warm welcome. The English Ambassador, William Trumbull, was told by Salisbury to keep a close eye on William, 'to observe how he is respected, to whom he mostly applies himself, who especially resort unto him, and what course he purposeth to take, either for his stay or his remove'. Mr Trumbull was also ordered by Salisbury 'to forbear both his conversation and his confidence. He was to be to him as a Gentile, so long as he doth remain a proselyte of that country, casting away that duty and obedience with which he was born, and betaking himself to protection in those parts.'[8]

Sir John More, in a letter to Winwood on 13 November 1611, states that the Archduke's Ambassador had behaved strangely since his arrival in England, and a letter from William to James expressed the hope that His Majesty would be pleased to pardon so small a fault as a clandestine marriage and to suffer his wife and him to live together.[9] Such correspondence did not improve matters: James always looked on the Archduke's court as the headquarters of Catholic interest in northern Europe.

A letter survives from Arbella to Queen Anne, probably written round about Christmas 1611, as she mentions James taking the holy sacrament around this time.

> May it please your most excellent Majesty to consider how long I have lived a spectacle of His Majesty's displeasure, to my unspeakable grief, and out of that gracious disposition which moved your royal mind to compassion of the distressed, may it please your Majesty to move his Majesty on my behalf. I have presumed to present your Majesty herewith the copy of my humble petition to his Majesty against this time, when the rather I am sure his Majesty forgiveth greater offences as freely as he desires to be forgiven by him whose sacrament he is to receive, though your Majesty's intercession at any time I know, were sufficient. Thus hath my long experience of your Majesty's gracious favour to me and all good causes encouraged me to presume to address myself to your Majesty, and increased the obligation of my duty in praying continually unto the Almighty for your Majesty's felicity in all things.[10]

However, such a petition would have had little or no weight with James, being advanced by a wife whom he rarely saw.

In January 1612 William heard from his grandfather that, provided he remained peacefully abroad, he would not be molested, another blow to Arbella's hopes of seeing him again. Lord Beauchamp died in July that year, and William's elder brother Edward assumed his courtesy title. Mary Shrewsbury came up for trial before the Star Chamber on 30 June. Salisbury, who had been suffering from cancer, died on 28 May, and Sir Francis Bacon was in charge of the proceedings. Mary was accused of contempt of court in refusing to speak at her examination. She still refused to discuss the escape and claimed her privilege to be tried by her peers. She was found guilty, fined £20,000 and confined in the Tower at the King's pleasure.

Soon after this, tragedy was to strike at the core of the House of

Stuart, deeply affecting the family and doing further damage to Arbella's hopes of a reprieve. Prince Henry had been under much pressure to marry, which caused him great concern, as he had showed little or no interest in women, as both Bacon and Cornwallis remarked. Catherine de' Medici was suggested as a possible bride, but Walter Raleigh, Henry's confidant, was against the match and advised him to bide his time. Meanwhile, Salisbury's death had had a profound effect on the Prince. He had always kept Henry informed of matters of state at home and abroad and allowed him to read ambassadorial dispatches.[11]

The Prince started to demonstrate signs of illness. He became very melancholy and retiring in his manner and complained of severe frontal headaches – once again, one of the symptoms of porphyria.[12] According to witnesses, he had 'heavy darkish looks, with a kind of mixture of melancholy and choler'.[13] He was often so weak and listless that he could not rise from his bed.

Dr Mayerne noted in the summer that when the King and Queen were staying with Henry at his house at Woodstock he suddenly became very ill, suffering attacks of fever, a vascular rash on his face resulting from exposure to the sun and inflammation of the lips and palms, symptoms very similar to those of his father. At the end of August Henry returned to Richmond, where he again felt very unwell. He was pale, depressed and sighed continually without knowing why. James must have noted these alarming symptoms in his son, so like his own, which would have added to his dynastic concerns in that, if Henry should die, there was only the weak Charles to inherit the throne, making any child that Arbella and William might have a threat.

By the beginning of October Henry's health began to deteriorate rapidly. Dr Hammond, his personal physician, who had been sent to examine Arbella in Barnet, could do little for him except to tell him to rest and remain quiet. Despite a violent attack of diarrhoea Henry set off to London to meet his sister's future husband, Frederick, the Elector of Palatine. He also dragged himself out of bed to play tennis, which made him so ill that he was unable to attend the banquet the Lord Mayor of London gave for the young couple. In rapid succession all the symptoms of porphyria overwhelmed him: diarrhoea, vomiting, rapid pulse, violent headaches, extreme weakness, sensitivity to light, laboured breathing, rigours, mounting delirium, 'alienation of the brain, ravings and idle speeches out of purpose, convulsions, coma and death'.[14]

Henry died on 6 November at eight o'clock at night. Dr Mayerne made sixteen pages of notes on Henry's illness but fell into such disfavour with James over his death that he later destroyed them. The death of the King's son and heir had a devastating effect on his health, and he became extremely ill soon afterwards, with 'melancholy', dread of everything, diarrhoea and persistent vomiting.

Arbella, who had been a close friend of Henry's until her attempted escape to France – which Henry had strongly disapproved of – must have been shattered by the news. And any chance of clemency from James was now even more remote.

Two months before Henry's death James had the body of his mother, Mary Queen of Scots, removed from its simple grave in Peterborough Cathedral to the splendid tomb in the Henry VII Chapel in Westminster Abbey where it remains today. Here the body of Prince Henry was placed beside his grandmother, accompanied by an outpouring of public grief at the loss of this young man who had shown such promise.

'WHAT MY BIRTH DID CLAIM
MY DEATH HATH PAID'

In March 1613 Arbella was ill with convulsions and very distracted. Dr Palmer was sent to her and found her 'out of frame' – that is, out of her mind.[1] In May the Lieutenant of the Tower, Sir William Waad, a vicious man, was removed from his post partly on the grounds of the many complaints made against him but also because he was found to have embezzled gold belonging to Arbella. His wife and daughter were also implicated in the crime, and the daughter was committed to the Tower on 19 May.[2] A third more reprehensible reason for his discharge was the plot afoot in the Howard camp, who were against Arbella and the Shrewsburys, to poison Sir Thomas Overbury, who was imprisoned in the Bloody Tower for speaking out against the divorce of Frances Howard and the Earl of Essex which took place to enable her to marry Somerset. Whatever else he may have been, Waad was an efficient gaoler, and while he was in charge there was little chance of such a plot succeeding. His replacement was Sir Gervase Elwes, a gentle man, who would give the plotters a greater chance of success. Indeed Overbury died of poisoning in the Tower in October 1613.

Arbella had hoped to be asked to the wedding of Princess Elizabeth to the Elector Frederick on 14 February 1613 and had cheered herself up by having four beautiful dresses made, one covered in £400 worth of pearls. Elizabeth tried to persuade her father to relent and let Arbella attend her wedding but to no avail. The authorities would not let Arbella out of the Tower.

Elwes's appointment inspired her friends, her aunt, Crompton and Reeves to try once more to help her escape. Arbella must have had considerable periods of lucidity at this time for her friends even to consider such a dangerous undertaking. If she had been acting irrationally they would never have contemplated it.

Arbella spent the first part of her imprisonment in the Lieutenant's Lodgings, a place from where it might have been possible to make an escape. Mary Shrewsbury was given permission to go home to nurse her sick husband, but her stay there was short once the new escape plans reached the ears of the members of the Privy Council.

All that winter of 1613 Arbella's spirits had been kept buoyant by the thought of escaping her confinement. Crompton, who had by this time been released from gaol, was in charge of her affairs, so he had access to her and began to pawn her remaining jewels. At this time Arbella was sane enough to direct her own affairs with his help – apart from during bouts of illness. She still had extravagant tastes in clothes and ornamentation and frequently purchased furniture and jewellery that she could not afford. In December she redeemed ten large pearls which had been pawned and bought some plate and a diamond ring. However, in July 1614 the plot to help her escape a second time was discovered. It was so secret that the details of the plot have never been made clear.

Crompton was committed once more to the Tower on 7 July with Dr Palmer. Arbella's servant Reeves was also implicated. The bitter disappointment of this second failure sent Arbella into another severe attack of depression, despair and illness from which she would never recover.

James was again very ill in the August of 1613, with uncontrollable vomiting, red-coloured urine and a tormenting pain in his left side. Dr Mayerne was afraid he would die and was so alarmed that he asked for four other physicians to be called.[3]

Arbella's last known letter, written around this time, is a desperate attempt to move the King to have pity on her. It is torn, blotted with tears and incomplete.

> In all humility, in most humble wise, the most wretched and unfortunate creature that ever lived prostrates herself at the feet of the most merciful king that ever was [even James should have felt some shame at this], desiring nothing but mercy and favour, not being more afflicted for anything than for the loss of that which hath been this long time the only comfort it had in the world, and which if it were to do again, I would not venture the loss of any for any other worldly comfort. Mercy it is that I desire and that for God's sake. Let either Freake or – [4]

Here the letter comes to an abrupt end but not before she has hinted that she has given up any thoughts of living with her husband again. Freake was her embroiderer and he had been involved in her escape from Hardwick. His devotion was another example of the remarkable loyalty that Arbella inspired in her servants – often to their cost. The letter was found in her room when she died.

William, who had by now moved from Bruges to Paris, had been told by the Privy Council that if he refrained from seditious behaviour he would be left in peace, to which he replied that he was grateful for that concession. This meant that he would not risk trying to contact his wife again without permission, not only for his sake but for hers. This news, when she found out about it, was a further blow to Arbella's hopes of ever seeing her husband again – or even hearing from him.

For the last year of her life tradition has it that she was removed to the Bell Tower, where she would remain until her death. The rooms there were considered to be some of the best in the Tower and had been occupied by Bishop John Fisher before his execution. Queen Elizabeth also lived in these lodgings before she became Queen. Catherine Grey, the wife of the Earl of Hertford, stayed in them, and it was here that Lord Beauchamp, Arbella's father-in-law, had been born fifty years earlier. The advantage of these chambers to those in charge of the prisoners was that there was no chance of escape. The only exit was through a narrow passage into the Governor's house. It was in the darker room below that Sir Thomas More spent the last days of his life. The upper chamber in which Arbella may have lodged had glass windows with views over the river to the south, Tower Hill to the north and the Lion Tower to the east. Her rooms were made moderately comfortable for her with carpets and wall hangings provided by her friends.

Arbella's last gift to her husband was a beautiful Book of Hours, given to her by Mary Queen of Scots and inscribed 'Your most unfortunate Arbella Seymour'. It was probably sent to William by the ever-faithful Crompton. At the time of the French Revolution, it was purchased in Paris by a Russian called Dubrowski and is now displayed in the Hermitage Museum in St Petersburg.

William has been criticized by historians such as Elizabeth Cooper for not helping his wife in her predicament. He proved to be a faithful and wise man in his later years, and, although very young at the time of his first marriage, he was shrewd enough to know that any attempt to free his wife would make James even more hostile towards her. A letter from an unknown correspondent to an unknown recipient in May 1613 states that William was angry with James for refusing to bestow his grace on him or to allow William and his wife to be reunited, thus shortening her life by the distraction of her mind. He was also deeply disappointed that his first submission to the Council had no effect and was determined to take some other course of action. In fact he never did, unless he was clandestinely involved in the failed 1614 plot to help Arbella escape.

In that year Dr Nicholas Felton was sent to Arbella to offer her spiritual comfort. He later became a great scholar and theologian and was known as a man of moderation, sound judgement and erudition. He was to become Master of Pembroke College, Cambridge, Bishop of Bristol and finally Bishop of Ely. It is possible that yet another rumour was circulating that she was about to convert to Roman Catholicism. To send such a renowned scholar to a sick and intermittently insane woman certainly seems a strange thing to do. Although all her life she had unwittingly been at the centre of various Catholic plots against James, she never gave any indication that she would convert to Catholicism, but James, in his paranoid state, may have been afraid that Arbella, having been so close to her Roman Catholic aunt, the Countess of Shrewsbury, might at last succumb to the Roman Church. Whatever James's reasons, Dr Felton was unable to give her spiritual comfort.

She took to her bed in despair and refused all medicine. Dr Moundford, who tried to save her life, wrote in her post-mortem notes that for a year before her death she would not even allow her doctors to feel her pulse or to examine her urine.[5] This last is significant, as Moundford would have taken a keen interest in the colour of her urine, since it was reported on by Dr Hammond when he examined her in Barnet. Both he and Dr Mayerne would have been well aware of the change in the colour of James's urine when he had attacks of his mysterious illness. Macalpine and Hunter, in their chapter on the Tudors and Stuarts in *George III and the Mad Business*, write, 'All the Victorian biographers of Arbella purged from their quotations all mention of urine both in her lifetime and in the post-mortem report without indication with the customary three ellipses that something had been omitted, and her later biographers to this day left it at that, obviously not having read the original sources.'[6] David Durant, who wrote his biography of Arbella after Macalpine's and Hunter's book appeared, did, however, quote the post-mortem report accurately.[7]

Anne Bradshaw, Arbella's servant from Hardwick days and her companion in her attempted escapes first from Hardwick and then Barnet, returned to her husband, an old servant of Bess, in Duffield, Derbyshire. Samuel Smith, who had become Arbella's servant on her marriage to William, took over many of Anne Bradshaw's duties, including dealing with visitors, and was with his mistress when she died.[8] He had proved invaluable to her in all sorts of ways during her sojourn with Sir Thomas Parry at Copt Hall in Lambeth, not least taking letters from her to her husband in the Tower. He was also with her in Barnet, carrying letters from Dr Moundford and her to the King and Privy Council. He was cross-examined at the time of her attempted escape to France, and when she first asked to have him as her servant in the Tower her request was refused.

Some time in 1615 Dr Mayerne stated that James was extremely ill with melancholia, persistent vomiting, red-tinted urine and severe pain in the left kidney, laboured breathing and diarrhoea. This bout of ill health was probably triggered by the summer weather, and he may also have been uncomfortably aware of public disapproval of his callous treatment of his dying cousin. The romance of her marriage to William – and the cruelty with which she had been treated afterwards – had caught the imagination of several ballad-makers and poets including Richard Corbet, Bishop of Norwich, who wrote movingly about her plight. After all, she was well known and much loved in the country as the King's next of kin after his children and, following Henry's death, her position as third in line to the throne.

Arbella refused all food during the last weeks of her life and became very thin. She was also in great pain. She finally died on 25 September 1615. Although her aunt was in the Tower, she was not with her at the time of death and was deeply upset when the news was conveyed to her.

A post-mortem was ordered on Arbella the following day. Sir Thomas Overbury's death in the Tower by poisoning was still uppermost in people's minds, and rumours of Arabella having been poisoned had to be nipped in the bud. The six doctors called on were the President of the Royal College of Surgeons himself, Dr William Paddy, Dr Edward Lister, Dr Richard Palmer, Dr John Argent, Dr Mathew Gwyn, all Fellows of the College, and Dr Moundford, who had looked after her for so many years. They found her body extremely emaciated and agreed that she had died of a chronic and long sickness but were unable to give it a name.

She was embalmed for the sum of £6 13s 4d, and her body was placed in a simple coffin. Unaccompanied by friends or relatives, she was carried out of her lodgings at dead of night on 27 September and taken up the river to Westminster Abbey. Here by the light of tapers a short burial service was read. Then, for the second time in three years, the tomb of Mary Queen of Scots was opened up and she was laid there with her aunt and cousin Prince Henry. Finally she was reunited with two of her favourite relatives. This meagre funeral for the King's cousin was deplored by his subjects. No stone was placed to mark her burial place. Years later a simple stone was laid on the floor by the tomb that states 'Arbella Stuart, 1575 to 1615', with no mention of her husband.

She lies very close to the magnificent tomb of her grandmother Margaret Lennox, which is in the entrance to the north aisle of the Henry VII Chapel, with her younger son Charles, Arbella's father, beside her. On the north side of the tomb is inscribed a roll of honour of Arbella's grandmother's forebears and relations. 'This lady herein had for her great grandfather King Edward IV, her father King Henry VII, her uncle King Henry VIII, her cousin germaine King Edward VI, her brother King James V of Scotland, her grandchild King James VI of Scotland. Her great-grandmother and grandmother were two Queens Elizabeth, her mother Margaret, Queen of Scots, her aunt Marie, the French Queen, her cousins germaine Queen Mary and Queen Elizabeth, and her niece and daughter-in-law Mary, Queen of Scots.'

Among the poems of Richard Corbet, Bishop of Norwich, is the following tribute to Arbella:

> How do I thank thee, Death, and bless thy power
> That I have passed the guard and 'scaped the Tower
> And now my pardon is my epitaph,
> And a small coffin my poor carcase hath;
> For at thy charge both soul and body were,
> Enlarged at last, secured from hope and fear,
> That among saints this amongst Kings is laid,
> And what my birth did claim my death hath paid.

EPILOGUE

Soon after Arbella's death rumours were flying about that she had given birth to a son by William while she was staying at Copt Hall in Lambeth with Sir Thomas Parry. The King and Privy Council took them very seriously and a commission was set up in 1616 to examine the matter. The commissioners were Ralph Winwood, Sir Francis Bacon and George Abbot, the Archbishop of Canterbury. Their task was a difficult one. All the main witnesses were devoted to Arbella, being either servants, friends or relatives. It is not surprising that they all denied any knowledge of any child, even if he indeed existed. Mary Shrewsbury and William were the chief witnesses; he denied the rumour and Mary refused to discuss it. Sir John Keys, Dr Moundford, Kirton and Reeves all agreed that, as far as they knew, no such child had been born. Mrs Bradshaw was living in Duffield, Derbyshire, and was too ill to travel to London, so the Clerk of the Council was sent down to interview her. She, too, denied any knowledge of a child, and at that point the matter was dropped. Mary Shrewsbury was sent back to the Tower for non-payment of the £20,000 fine, where she remained from 1618 to 1623. During this time, when questioned once more on the subject, she admitted that she did not think that Arbella had ever given birth to a baby.[1]

The existence of such a child was by no means impossible, however. She and William were certainly able to meet while she was at Copt Hall, and a child born there could have been spirited away to safety. If such an infant had existed – and survived and married – he or she would have inherited Arbella's royal lineage and also the porphyria that so blighted her life.

After Arbella's death there was no reason for William to remain in exile. In 1616 he returned home and was soon restored to favour. That November he was indeed made a Knight of the Bath on the installation of Prince Charles as Prince of Wales. In 1617 he married as his second wife Frances Devereux, daughter of Arbella's first love, Robert, Earl of Essex. He named his first daughter of this marriage Arbella. She died unmarried and is buried beside him in the parish church of St Mary the Virgin at Great Bedwyn in Wiltshire. He took Arbella's servants Hugh Crompton and Edward Kirton into his household, and they both became Members of Parliament in the 1620s. Crompton died in 1645 and Kirton in 1654. Both are buried in the church at Great Bedwyn.

NOTES

Chapter 1
1. Statutes of the Realm, Henry VIII, Vol. XXIV, p. 31.
2. State Papers, Domestic, Elizabeth, Vol. XXXVI, p. 25.
3. Zurich Letters, Second Series, p. 200.
4. State Papers, Domestic, Elizabeth, 1574, Vol. XCIV, p. 12.
5. Howard Collection of Letters, pp. 235–7.
6. Lodge's *Illustrations of British History*, Vol. II, p. 122.
7. Harleian MSS, Vol. 588, fols 13, 23.
8. State Papers, Mary Queen of Scots, Vol. X, p. 71.
9. Harleian MSS, Vol. 289, fol. 196.
10. Harleian MSS, Vol. 289, fols 200, 202.

Chapter 2
1. Calendar of State Papers, Scottish Series, Mary Queen of Scots, Vol. XII, fol. 83.
2. State Papers, Domestic, Elizabeth, Vol. CCXXX, fol. 99.
3. *William Tytler's Enquiry*, Vol. II, p. 70.
4. Agnes Strickland, *Lives of the Queens of Scotland and English Princesses*, Vol. 2, 1851, p. 417.
5. *Ellis's Letters*, 2rd Series, Vol. II, p. 60.
6. Lansdown MSS, Vol. 34, fol. 1.
7. Robert Douglas, *Peerage of Scotland*, 1764, Vol. II, pp. 98, 99.
8. State Papers, Domestic, Elizabeth, Vol. CLIII, fol. 39.
9. Ida Macalpine and Richard Hunter, 'Porphyria in the Royal Houses of Stuart, Hanover and Prussia', *British Medical Journal*, 1968, Vol. I (January), pp. 7–18.
10. Historical Manuscripts Commission, Vol. III, p. 42.
11. J. Morris, *Letters and Books of Sir Amyas Paulet*, 1874.
12. Lansdown MSS, Vol. 34, p. 145.

Chapter 3

1. Joseph Hunter, *Hallamshire: The History and Topography of the Parish of Sheffield in the County of York*, 1875, p. 118.
2. Sir John Harrington. *A Tract on the Succession to the Crown*, 1602 (1880).
3. State Papers, Domestic, Elizabeth, Vol. CCXXXIII, p. 73.
4. State Papers, Scottish Series, Elizabeth, Vol. XLVII, p. 123.
5. Lansdown MSS, Vol. 71, fol. 2; *Ellis's Letters*, 2rd Series, Vol. VII, p. 165.
6. David N. Durant, *Arbella Stuart*, pp. 61–2.
7. Sully's *Mémoires*, Vol. II, p. 70.
8. Nicholl's *Progresses*, Vol. III, p. 451.

Chapter 4

1. Lindsay Boynton (ed.), *Hardwick Hall Inventories of 1601*, Furniture Society, London, 1971.
2. Cecil Papers, Vol. 135, fol. 175.
3. Foley Records, Vol. I, p. 43.
4. Cecil Papers, Vol. 135, fol. 107.
5. Cecil Papers, Vol. 135, fol. 123.
6. Cecil Papers, Vol. 135, fol. 128.
7. Cecil Papers, Vol. 135, fol. 147.

Chapter 5

1. Cecil Papers, Vol. 135, fol. 170.
2. Cecil Papers, Vol. 135, fol. 147.
3. Cecil Papers, Vol. 92, fol. 1.
4. Cecil Papers, Vol. 135, Holograph 142.
5. Cecil Papers, Vol. 135, Vol. 135, fols 159, 160.
6. Cecil Papers, Vol. 135, fol. 164.
7. Cecil Papers, Vol. 135, fol. 130.
8. Röhl, Warner and Hunt, *Purple Secret*, pp. 297, 306.

Chapter 6

1. Cecil Papers, Vol. 135, fol. 174.
2. Sloane MSS, Vol. 718.
3. Hatfield Papers, Vol. XV, fol. 65.
4. Hatfield Papers, Vol. XV, fol. 82.
5. Cecil Papers, Vol. 100, fol. 134.
6. Lodge's *Illustrations*, Vol. III, pp. 176–8.

7. Lodge's *Illustrations*, Vol. III, pp. 214–21.

8. Sloane MSS, Vol. 4164, fol. 181.

9. Sloane MSS, Vol. 4164, fol. 183.

10. Lodge's *Illustrations*, Vol. III, p. 182.

11. Sloane MSS, Vol. 4164, fols 181, 182.

12. Sloane MSS, Vol. 4164, fol. 187.

13. Sloane MSS, Vol. 4164, pp. 188–91.

Chapter 7

1. The origin of this letter cannot be traced, although it is quoted in Elizabeth Cooper's *The Life and Letters of Lady Arbella Stuart*. Dr James Montague became Bishop of Winchester in 1616.

2. Harleian MSS, Vol. 6986, fol. 71.

3. Harleian MSS, Vol. 7003, fol. 45.

4. Harleian MSS, Vol. 7003, fol. 46.

5. Harleian MSS, Vol. 6986, fol. 74.

6. Harleian MSS, Vol. 6986, fol. 76.

7. Harleian MSS, Vol. 7003, fol. 38.

8. Sloane MSS, Vol. 4164, fol. 194.

9. Hugh Crompton's Accounts, Seymour Papers, Longleat, Vol. XXII; Canon Jackson's *Wiltshire Archaeological Magazine*, Vol. XIX, pp. 217–26.

Chapter 8

1. State Papers, Domestic, James I, Vol. LXIX, p. 42.

2. Ralph Winwood, *Memorials of the Affairs of State*, Vol. III, p. 117.

3. Sloane MSS, Vol. 1679, fols 19v, 21r, 23r, 26v.

4. Antonia Fraser, *Mary Queen of Scots*, p. 445.

5. Ralph Winwood, *Memorials of the Affairs of State*, Vol. III, p. 119.

6. Harleian MSS, Vol. 7003, fol. 59.

7. Benjamin Disraeli, *Curiosities of Literature* (13th edn), p. 360.

8. Canon Jackson, *Wiltshire Archaeological Magazine*, Vol. XIX, p. 201.

9. State Papers, Domestic, James I, Vol. LIII, p. 55.

10. Susan Cole, 'So Sweet a Star as Harry', *Stuart Papers*, 1992, no. XXXIX.

11. Nichol's *Progresses of Queen Elizabeth and James I*, Vol. II, p. 348.

12. Harleian MSS, Vol. 7003, fol. 62.

13. Canon Jackson, *Wiltshire Archaeological Magazine*, Vol. XV, p. 201.

Chapter 9

1. Harleian MSS, Vol. 7003, fol. 111.
2. Harleian MSS, Vol. 7003, fol. 62.
3. Harleian MSS, Vol. 7003, fol. 71.
4. Harleian MSS, Vol. 7003, fol 92.
5. State Papers, Domestic, James I, Vol. LVI, p. 56.
6. Lansdown MSS Vol. 1236, fol. 58.
7. State Papers: Domestic, James I, Vol.LVII, p. 118.
8. Harleian MSS, Vol. 7003, fol. 82.
9. Harleian MSS, Vol. 7003, fol. 64.
10. Harleian MSS, Vol. 7003, fol. 64.
11. Harleian MSS, Vol. 7003, fol. 150.
12. *Lives of the Friends of Clarendon*, Vol. 3, p. 148.
13. Harleian MSS, Vol. 7003, fol. 152; Sloane MSS, Vol. 4161, fol. 46.
14. State Papers, James I, Vol. LXII, fol. 88.
15. Harleian MSS, Vol. 7003, fols 94, 96, 97.
16. State Papers, Domestic, James I, Vol. LXI, p. 30.
17. Harleian MSS, Vol. 7003, fol. 102.
18. Percy Lovell, *The Village of Highgate: Part I*, London: London County Council, 1936 (reprinted as *Highgate*, John Richardson Historical Publications, 1983). (In 1889 the owner, Sir Sidney Waterlow, Bt, my great-great-grandfather-in-law, presented the house and park to the London County Council.

Chapter 10

1. Harleian MSS, Vol. 7003, fol. 116.
2. Sloane MSS, Vol. 4121, fol. 57.
3. Harleian MSS, Vol. 7003, fol. 89.
4. Frederick Cass, *The Parish of East Barnet*.
5. State Papers, Domestic, James I, Vol. LXVII, p. 30.
6. State Papers, Domestic, James I, Vol. LXVII, p. 38.
7. Harleian MSS, Vol. 7003, fol. 118.
8. Harleian MSS, Vol. 7003, fol. 118.
9. Sloane MSS, Vol. 4161, fol. 61.
10. Sloane MSS, Vol. 4161, fol. 68.
11. Sloane MSS, Vol. 2063, fols 18–33.
12. Ralph Winwood, *Memorials of the Affairs of State*, Vol. III, p. 280.
13. John Bright's examination, State Papers, Domestic, James I, Vol. LXIV, p. 30.

14. Harleian MSS, Vol. 7003, fol. 22.
15. State Papers, Domestic, James I, Vol. LXIV, p. 4.
16. Thomas Rymer's *Fædera*, Vol. 16, p. 710.
17. Harleian MSS, Vol. 7003, fol. 132.

Chapter 11

1. State Papers, Domestic, James I, Vol LXIV, p. 4.
2. Harleian MSS, Vol. 7003, fol. 128.
3. Harleian MSS, Vol. 7003, fol. 130.
4. Harleian MSS, Vol. 7003, fol. 140.
5. Ralph Winwood, *Memorials of the Affairs of State*, Vol. III, p. 281.
6. Sloane MSS, Vol. 2063, fols 18–33.
7. Sloane MSS, Vol. 4161, fol. 63.
8. Ralph Winwood, *Memorials of the Affairs of State*, Vol. III, p. 282; Sloane MSS, Vol. 4161, fol. 32.
9. Ralph Winwood, *Memorials of the Affairs of State*, Vol. III, p. 301.
10. Harleian MSS, Vol. 7003, fol. 78.
11. Susan Cole, 'So Sweet a Star as Harry', *Stuart Papers*, 1992, no. XXXIX.
12. J.H. Jesse, *Memoirs of the Court of England in the Time of the Stuarts*, Vol. 1, p. 168.
13. G. Goodman, *Court of James I*, Vol. 1, ed. J.S. Brewer, p. 237.
14. F. Peek, *Desiderata Curiosa*, Vol. 1, pp. 199–204.

Chapter 12

1. Calendar of State Papers, 1611–18, pp. 16, 242.
2. Calendar of State Papers, 1611–18, p. 185.
3. Calendar of State Papers, 1611–18, p. 185.
4. Harleian MSS, Vol. 7113, fol. 146.
5. Historical Commission, Eighth Report, Part I, pp. 228b, 229.
6. Macalpine and Hunter, *George III and the Mad Business*, p. 219.
7. David N. Durant, *Arbella Stuart*, p. 207.
8. Ralph Winwood, *Memorials of the Affairs of State*, Vol. III, p. 200.

Epilogue

1. State Papers, Domestic, James I, Vol. XCIV, p. 126.

BIBLIOGRAPHY

Archaeological Magazine, Wiltshire, Vol. XV, p. 201; Vol. XIX, pp. 217–26.

Bradley, E.T., *Life of the Lady Arabella Stuart* (2 vols), Richard Bentley and Son, London, 1889

Calendar of State Papers, Scottish Series, Vols XII, XLVI

Calendar of State Papers, 1611–18

Cecil Papers, Historical Manuscript Commission Reports, 1883

Cole, Susan, 'So Sweet a Star as Harry', *Stuart Papers*, 1992, No. XXXIX, Royal Stuart Society, London

Cooper, Elizabeth, *The Life and Letters of Lady Arabella Stuart*, Hurst and Blackett, London, 1866

Costello, L.S., *Memoirs of Eminent English Women*, Richard Bentley, London, 1844

Disraeli, Benjamin, *Curiosities of Literature*, Richard Bentley, London, 1838

Douglas, Robert, *Peerage of Scotland*, Vol. 2, R. Fleming, Edinburgh, 1764

Durant, David N., *Arbella Stuart: A Rival to the Queen*, Weidenfeld and Nicolson, London, 1978

Durant, David N., *Bess of Hardwick*, Weidenfeld and Nicolson, 1977; reissued by Peter Owen, London, 1999

Ellis, John, *Letters*, Second Series, Vols 2, 8, 12, Henry Cobourne, London, 1829.

Foley, Henry, *Records of the English Province of the Society of Jesus*, Vol. I, Burns and Oates, London, 1877

Fraser, Antonia, *Mary Queen of Scots*, Weidenfeld and Nicolson, London, 1969

Fraser, Antonia, *King James VI of Scotland, I of England*, Weidenfeld and Nicholson, London, 1974

Gear, Gillian, 'Lady Arbella Stuart and East Barnet', *Barnet and District Local History Bulletin*, No. 36, London, November 1999

Goodman, Godfrey, *The Court of King James I*, ed. J.S. Brewer, Richard Bentley, London, 1839

Handover, P.M., *Arbella Stuart*, Eyre and Spottiswoode, London, 1957

Hardy, B.C., *Arbella Stuart*, Constable and Co., London, 1913

Harleian MSS, Vols 289, 588, 6986, 7003, British Museum

Harrington, Sir John, *Tract on Successors to the Crown 1602*, printed privately, 1880

Historical Commission MSS, Report III, 1880

Houston, S.J., *James I*, Longman, London, 1973

Howard, Leonard, *Letters* (private printing), E. Withers, London, 1753

Hunter, Joseph, *Hallamshire: The History and Topography of the Parish of Sheffield in the County of Yorkshire*, Virtue and Co., London, 1875

Inderwick, F.A., *Sidelights on the Stuarts*, Samson Low, Marston, Searle and Rivington, London, 1888

Jesse, J.H., *Memoirs of the Court of England in the Time of the Stuarts*, Richard Bentley, London, 1840

Lewis, Lady Thérèse, *Lives of the Friends and Contemporaries of Lord Chancellor Clarendon* (3 vols), John Murray, London, 1852

Lockyer, Roger, *James VI and I*, Longman, London, 1998

Lodge, Edmund, *Illustrations of British History*, C. Nicol, London, 1791

Macalpine, Ida and Richard Hunter, *George III and the Mad Business*, Pimlico, London, 1969

Macalpine, Ida and Richard Hunter, 'Porphyria in the Royal Houses of Stuart, Hanover and Prussia', *British Medical Journal*, 1963, Vol. I (January), pp. 7–18

Moore, Norman, *Medicine in the British Isles*, Clarendon Press, Oxford, 1908

Morris, J., *Letters and Books of Sir Myas Paulet*, Burns and Oates, London, 1874

Nichol, John, *Nichol's Progresses*, Printer to the Society of Antiquaries, London, 1788

Peek, F., *Desiderata Curiosa*, Thomas Evans, London, 1779

Richardson, John, *The Village of Highgate*, Historical Publications, London, 1983

Röhl, John, Martin Warren and David Hunt, *Purple Secret: Genes, Madness and the Royal Houses of Europe*, Bantam Press, London, 1998

Rymer, Thomas, *Fœdera*, Apud Joannem Nexulme, The Hague, 1806

Seymour Papers, Longleat, Wiltshire

Sloane MSS, British Museum

State Papers, Domestic, Elizabeth, Vols CCIII, CCXXXI

State Papers, Domestic, James I, Vol. LVIV

Statutes of the Realm, Vol. XXIV, Public Record Office

Strickland, Agnes, *Lives of the Queens of Scotland and English Princesses*, William Blackwood, Edinburgh and London, 1850

Tytler, William, *Inquiry into the Evidence Against Mary Queen of Scots*, Edinburgh, 1759

Winwood, Ralph, *Memorials of the Affairs of State in the Reign of Queen Elizabeth and King James I* (3 vols), T. Ward, London, 1725

INDEX

Abbot, George, Archbishop of
  Canterbury, 149
Adam, Mrs (of East Barnet), 128,
  137
Adventure (ship), 135–6
Agard, Frances, 20
Albert, Prince Consort, 70
Alexandra, Tsarina of Russia, 70
Alien Act, 16, 24, 103
Angus, Archibald Douglas, 6th Earl
  of, 16
Anhault, Prince of, 85
Anne Boleyn, Queen of Henry VIII,
  16
Anne of Denmark, Queen of James
  I: marriage, 38; arrives at Windsor,
  77; devotion to Arbella, 77, 79, 84;
  New Year gift from Arbella, 82;
  illness during brother Christian's
  visit, 90; coolness to Arbella, 91–2;
  presents and performs in masques,
  93, 105; letters from Arbella during
  house arrest, 110–12; letter from
  Arbella in Tower asking for James's
  clemency, 140
Arenberg, Count (Austrian
  Ambassador), 78
Argent, Dr John, 147
Arundel, Anne, Countess of, 93
Aston, near Sheffield, 95

Aubespine de Châteauneuf, Claude
  d', 41
Aubespine de Châteauneuf, Madame
  d', 40

Babington, Anthony: correspondence
  with Mary Queen of Scots, 39
Bacon, Sir Francis, 140–1, 149
Baisley, John, 137
Barlow, Robert (Bess of Hardwick's
  first husband), 19
Barnet, 117–19, 121, 123–7
Bartie, Mr (Duchess of Suffolk's
  husband), 22
Batten, Thomas, 129, 137
Baynton, Mr (friend of Arbella and
  Seymour), 100, 102
Beale, Robert, 28
Beaton, James, Archbishop of
  Glasgow, 30
Beauchamp, Edward Seymour,
  Baron (Earl of Hertford's son): as
  prospective husband for Arbella,
  55, 75; in line to throne, 103; death,
  140; birth in Tower, 145
Beauchamp, Edward Seymour,
  Baron (son of above) *see* Seymour,
  Edward
Beaulieu, James, 100
Bedford, Lucy, Countess of, 84

Bess of Hardwick *see* Shrewsbury,
Elizabeth Talbot, Countess of
Biron, Mrs (Arbella's servant), 106
Blackfriars: Arbella buys house at, 94
Blague, Revd John, 106–7
Bond, Sir William, 117–18, 121
Bothwell, James Hepburn, 4th Earl
of, 18, 30
Bowes, Isobel, Lady (*later* Lady
Darcy), 95, 97
Bowyer, Sir William, 138
Bradshaw, Anne, 106, 127–9, 132,
146–7, 149
Bright, John, 129, 135
Brooke, Lord George, 79–80
Brounker, Sir Henry: interrogates
Arbella, 58–9, 62–4; letters from
Arbella, 64–7, 73, 76, 80;
investigates Arbella's escape plot
from Hardwick, 74
Bruges, 139
Buggs, Mr (of Fleet Street), 100, 102
Bulkeley, Sir Richard, 58
Burghley, William Cecil, Baron: and
detention of Arbella's Lennox
grandparents, 17; letters from 6th
Earl of Shrewsbury, 23–4; defends
Arbella's claim to Earldom, 25;
Countess of Lennox describes
porphyria symptoms to, 30; 7th
Earl of Shrewsbury writes to on
death of Arbella's mother, 31; Bess
writes to requesting continuation of
Arbella's allowance, 32–4;
entertains Arbella, 41; warns Bess
of dangers to Arbella, 46; and
Arbella's claim to throne, 48
Buxton, 95

Bye Plot, 79–80

Caesar, Sir Julius, 118
Campion, Father Edward, 21, 35–6
Catherine of Aragon, Queen of
Henry VIII, 16
Catherine de' Medici, Queen of
France, 141
Catholics: plot to kidnap Arbella, 45,
48
Cavendish, Catherine (*née* Ogle;
Charles's wife), 21, 61
Cavendish, Charles (Bess of
Hardwick's son): marriage, 21;
stands godfather to Arbella, 24;
sides with mother in matrimonial
quarrels, 35; dispute with
stepfather over land, 38–9; presents
Arbella to Queen Elizabeth, 40;
debts, 84; Arbella finds place at
court for, 85; and mother's death,
94
Cavendish, Elizabeth (*née* Parker;
William's second wife), 20
Cavendish, George, 19
Cavendish, Grace (Henry's wife), 21,
35, 57, 83
Cavendish, Henry (Bess's eldest son):
marriage, 21, 35; sides with
stepfather in matrimonial disputes,
35, 39; evicted from Chatsworth,
39; and Arbella's marriage
prospects, 56–7; rift with mother,
63; supports Arbella in bid to
escape from Hardwick, 73–4, 83;
excluded from Bess's will, 74;
suspected of implication in Main
Plot, 81; Shrewsburys seek

reconciliation with, 83

Cavendish, Margaret (*née* Bostock; William's first wife), 20

Cavendish, Sir William (Bess of Hardwick's second husband), 19–20

Cavendish, William (Bess of Hardwick's son) *see* Devonshire, 1st Earl of

Cecil, Sir Robert *see* Salisbury, 1st Earl of

Cecil, William *see* Burghley, Baron

Chamberlain, John, 98

Chandos, Frances, Lady, 126–7

Chapman, Christopher, 73–4

Charles I, King of England: passes on 70

porphyria, 70; made Duke of Albany and knighted, 87; poor health, 90, 141; and succession to father, 141

Charles (ship), 132

Charlotte, Princess (Queen Victoria's granddaughter), 70

Chatsworth House: Arbella born in, 15; William Cavendish purchases, 20; rebuilt and improved, 21, 37; Bess of Hardwick owns and occupies, 27, 34; Mary Queen of Scots at, 37; Shrewsburys' dispute over, 39

Chaworth, George, 66–7

Chaworth, Mary (*née* Kniverton), 66, 138

Cheneys, Joan, Lady, 95

Cholmeley, Sir Jasper, 121

Cholmeley, Katherine (*née* Pym), 121

Cholmeley, William, 121

Christian IV, King of Denmark, 90–2

Christopher, Father Thomas, 45

Clarendon, Edward Hyde, 1st Earl of, 100

Clarke, Father, 79

Cobham, Henry Brooke, 8th Baron, 80

Cockett, Griffin, 135

Coke, Sir Edward, 81

Collingwood, Alice, 115

Collingwood, Francis, 115

Conyers, Thomas, 121, 128

Cook (7th Earl of Shrewsbury's steward), 84

Coombe Abbey, 89

Cooper, Elizabeth, 145

Copt Hall, near Vauxhall, 94, 108–9, 149

Corbet, Richard, Bishop of Norwich, 147–8

Cornwallis, Sir Charles, 141

Corvé, Tassin, 137

Crofts, Sir James, 118, 121–4, 131, 137–8

Crompton, Hugh: and costs of Arbella's progress, 95; records Arbella's marriage to William Seymour, 106; imprisoned after Arbella's marriage, 107, 109; and Arbella's stay at Highgate, 118; in Arbella's escape plot, 127–9, 131; further imprisonments and torture, 137, 144; and Arbella's second escape plan, 143; pawns Arbella's jewels, 144; sends Arbella's final gift to William, 145; later career and death, 150

Cutting, Francis ('Thomas'), 91–2

Darcy, John, Lord, 95

Darnley, Henry Stuart, Earl of:
relationship to Arbella, 15; birth,
17; marriage to Mary Queen of
Scots, 17–18, 137; killed, 18, 22–3,
32

Denbigh, Robert Dudley, Baron:
childhood engagement to Arbella
and death, 38

Devonshire, William Cavendish, 1st
Earl of (Bess of Hardwick's son):
upbringing, 21; supports mother in
matrimonial disputes, 35; dispute
with stepfather over land and
property, 38–9; inherits Hardwick
Hall, 38; searches for Harrison, 47;
at Hardwick Hall, 53, 66; and
Arbella's marriage prospects, 56;
barony, 87–8, 93–4; at Princess
Mary's christening, 88–9; behaviour
at mother's death, 93–4

Devonshire, William Cavendish, 4th
Earl and 1st Duke of, 37

Disraeli, Benjamin, 102

Dodderidge, John, 57–8

Douglas, Margaret see Lennox,
Margaret, Countess of

Dove, Henry, 73–4

Drummond, Jane, Lady, 111

Dunfermline, Abbot of, 30

Dunfermline, Alexander Seton, 1st
Earl of, 104

Durant, David, 146

Durham: Arbella banished to,
115–18, 122–4

Easton Maudit, near
Wellingborough, 95

Edmondes, Sir Thomas, 100

Edward VI, King of England (earlier
Prince; Henry VIII's son): birth, 17;
favours Sir William Cavendish, 20

Elizabeth I, Queen of England:
succession to, 15, 24, 33, 48–9, 74;
birth, 16; hostility to Mary Queen
of Scots, 17; Bess of Hardwick
serves, 20; disapproves of marriage
of Elizabeth and Charles Lennox,
22–3; pleads for restoration of
Arbella's title, 25; pays for
Margaret Lennox's funeral, 29;
allowances to Arbella and mother,
31–4; and Arbella's marriage
prospects, 38, 44, 48, 56; invites
Arbella to dine, 40–1; and trial and
execution of Mary Queen of Scots,
40; displeased with Arbella's
behaviour, 43; exchanges gifts with
Arbella, 49; banishes Arbella, 50;
and Hertford's marriage to
Catherine Grey, 55–6; anger at
Arbella's plan to marry Edward
Seymour, 57–9; health decline, 58,
62, 69, 74; mourns death of Essex,
69; death and burial, 74–5; lives in
Tower of London's Bell Tower, 145

Elizabeth, Princess (later Queen of
Bohemia), 77, 89, 105, 143

Elwes, Sir Gervase, 143

Essex, Frances, Countess of see
Howard, Lady Frances

Essex, Robert Devereux, 2nd Earl of:
relations with Arbella, 50–1, 67–8;
death, 54, 67, 69; daughter Frances
marries William Seymour, 149–50

Essex, Robert Devereux, 3rd Earl of,
143

Facton, Mr (of Hucknell), 73–4

Farnese, Rainutio, 45

Farnham family, 95

Fawkes, Guy, 98

Felton, Nicholas (*later* Bishop of Ely), 146

Fenton, Elizabeth, Viscountess (*née* Pierrepoint; Frances' daughter), 27, 138–9

Fenton, Thomas Erskine, 1st Viscount, 27, 115, 138–9

Feodora, Grand Duchess (Queen Victoria's great-granddaughter), 70

Fisher, John, Bishop of Rochester, 145

Flodden, Battle of (1515), 16

Foljambe, Godfrey, 95

Fotheringhay Castle, Northamptonshire, 40

Fowler, Thomas, 24, 29, 81

Fowler, Sir William, 81

Francis I, King of France, 17

Francis II, King of France: betrothal to Mary Queen of Scots, 17

Freake (Arbella's embroiderer), 73, 144–5

Frederick V, Elector Palatine (*later* King of Bohemia), 141, 143

Gal, Udo, 91

Garnet, Father Henry, 69, 90

George III, King, 70

Gloucester, Prince William of, 70

Greville, George, 70

Grey, Lady Catherine (Countess of Hertford), 55–6, 67, 103, 107, 113, 145

Grey, Elizabeth *see* Kent, Countess of

Grey, Lady Jane, 19, 55, 57

Grey, Sir John *see* Kent, 5th Earl of

Grey of Wilton, Thomas, 15th Baron, 80

Gunpowder Plot (1605), 89–90

Hammond, Dr John, 119–20, 141, 146

Hampton Court, 82

Hardwick Hall, Derbyshire: Arbella stays in as child, 27–8; Bess acquires and rebuilds, 37–8; Thomas Morley at, 48; Arbella confined in, 53–9, 64–6, 69; described, 53–4; Arbella plans escape from, 73

Hardwick, John, 19

Harrington, John, 1st Baron, and Anne, Lady, 89

Harrington, Sir John, 44, 50, 94

Harrison (seminarist), 47

Hawkins, John, 104

Henry IV, King of France, 48–9; assassinated, 104

Henry VII, King of England, 16

Henry VIII, King of England: lacks male heir, 15; marriages and children, 16–17; gives property to Margaret Douglas (Lennox), 66

Henry, Prince of Wales (eldest son of James I): death from porphyria, 9, 71, 99, 141–2; birth, 48; liking for and friendship with Arbella, 77, 89, 98; and Arbella's relinquishing Cutting's service to Danish king, 92; invested as Prince of Wales, 104–5; concern for Arbella on journey to Durham, 122–3, 126; Arbella buried beside, 148

Hertford, Edward Seymour, 1st Earl of: marriage to Catherine Grey, 55–6, 103, 107, 113; proposed marriage of son and grandson to Arbella, 57, 59; Elizabeth's attitude to, 67, 69; and Arbella's marriage to William, 105–7, 113; dislikes Rodney, 105–6; and James' illness, 114; and escape of Arbella and William, 130, 136–7

Highgate, 117–18

Holford (Cecils' spy), 67

Hopton, Sir Owen, 56

Howard, Lady Frances (Countess of Essex; *later* Countess of Somerset), 143

Howard, Lord Henry, 50

Howard, Lord Thomas, 16–17

Hucknell, Derbyshire, 73

Huntingdon, Henry Hastings, 3rd Earl of, 24

Jackson, Canon John Edward, 102, 106

James I, King of England (James VI of Scotland): death from porphyria, 9, 70; deprecates Arbella's marriage to Seymour, 9, 95, 98; as Arbella's first cousin, 15; claims to succession to English throne, 15, 28, 30, 48–9; birth, 18; succeeds to Scots throne, 18; Margaret Lennox visits, 22; and Lennox earldom, 25, 32; appropriates Arbella's jewellery inheritance, 30; Elizabeth suggests as husband for Arbella, 38; marriage to Anne of Denmark, 38; and execution of mother (Mary Queen of Scots), 40; writes to Arbella, 45–6; and Arbella's attachment to Essex, 69; inconsistent treatment of Arbella, 69; porphyria symptoms, 69, 99, 112, 144, 146–7; succeeds Elizabeth as king of England, 74; concern for Arbella at beginning of reign, 75–7; hunting, 75, 84, 89, 114; journey south on accession, 75; requests Kent to take Arbella into home, 75–6; pays pension and allowance to Arbella, 78, 85, 98, 138; and plots to entice Arbella away and place on English throne, 79; New Year gift from Arbella, 82; refuses Arbella permission to wed, 85, 93; correspondence with Bess over receiving Arbella, 88; relations with son Henry, 89; and Gunpowder Plot, 90; grants monopoly on oats to Arbella, 94; Arbella petitions for increase in allowance, 97; deteriorating relations with Arbella, 98–9; grants Arbella permission to marry a loyal subject, 98, 100, 111; dissolves Parliament (1610), 100; William Seymour makes submission to on betrothal to Arbella, 101–3; hereditary rights to English throne ratified (1604), 103; Arbella petitions during house arrest, 109–11, 114; ill health, 114; banishes Arbella to Durham, 115–16, 123–4; scepticism over Arbella's ill health on journey to Durham, 119–20, 125–6; Bishop of Durham reports to on Arbella,

122–3; grants Arbella one month's respite on journey to Durham, 122; Arbella pleads with for more time to recover, 124–5; vesicular rash, 127; reaction to Arbella's escape to France, 131–2, 134; unrelenting attitude towards Arbella, 138, 140; and William Seymour's stay in Bruges, 140; and son Henry's illness and death, 141–2; Arbella's final known letter to pleads for pity, 144; fears Arbella's conversion to Catholicism, 146

James IV, King of Scots, 16

James V, King of Scots, 16, 70

James, William, Bishop of Durham, 115–18, 122–3, 125

Jane Seymour, Queen of Henry VIII, 55–7

Jesuits: influence on Mary Queen of Scots, 35; and Arbella's claim to throne, 48; *see also* Catholics

Johnstone, Nathaniel, 82

Jonson, Ben: *Masque of Queens*, 95

Kent, Elizabeth, Countess of (*née* Talbot), 74, 96

Kent, Sir John Grey, 5th Earl of, 56, 74–6, 96

Keys, Sir John, 149

Kinloss, Edward Bruce, 1st Baron, 94

Kirton, Edward, 56, 106, 118, 137, 149–50

Knyevet, Elizabeth, Lady (*née* Hayward), 18, 98

Knyevet, Thomas, Baron, 98

Kynnersley, Nicholas, 43

Langside, Battle of (1568), 18

Lauderdale House, Highgate, 118

Lea, Sir Henry, 78

Leche, Alice (*née* Hardwick; Bess of Hardwick's sister), 20

Leche, Elizabeth (*earlier* Hardwick; Bess of Hardwick's mother), 20

Leche, Francis, 20

Leche, John, 20

Leche, Ralph, 20

Leicester, Robert Dudley, 1st Earl of, 23, 38–9

Lennox, Charles Stuart, 5th Earl of (Arbella's father): birth, 17; and mother's imprisonment, 18; courtship and marriage, 19, 21–4; succeeds to earldom, 19, 25; upbringing, 19; death, 25; and James's appropriation of earldom, 32; tomb, 148

Lennox, Elizabeth, Countess of (*née* Cavendish; Arbella's mother): and Arbella's birth, 15, 24; courtship and marriage, 19, 21–4; and disinheritance of Arbella, 25; allowance from Queen Elizabeth, 31; death, 31

Lennox, Esmé, Stuart, 1st Duke of (Seigneur d'Aubigny), 32, 48, 88

Lennox, Margaret, Countess of (*née* Douglas; Arbella's grandmother): birth and upbringing, 16; imprisoned, 16–17, 137; and succession to English throne, 16–17; detained by Queen Elizabeth, 17–18; marriage and children, 17; Bess of Hardwick meets, 21; and daughter Elizabeth's

marriage, 21–4; renews friendship
with Mary Queen of Scots, 24–5;
and disinheritance of Arbella, 25;
death and debts, 28–30, 34; leaves
Smallwood to Arbella, 35, 66;
tomb, 148

Lennox, Matthew Stuart, 4th Earl of
(Arbella's grandfather): imprisoned
by Elizabeth, 17–18; marriage, 17;
made Regent of Scotland, 18;
murdered, 18–19; and earldom
succession, 25, 32

Lister, Sir Edward, 147

Lumley, John, 6th Baron, 104

Macalpine, Ida and Richard Hunter:
on porphyria, 36, 69, 146

Main, or Spanish Plot, 79–80

Malliet (Charles Lennox's tutor), 19

Manners family, 35

Mansfield, Derbyshire, 73

Mar, John Erskine, 1st or 6th Earl of,
18, 77

Margaret Tudor, Queen of James IV
of Scotland (*later* Countess of
Angus; Henry VIII's eldest sister),
15–16, 70

Marguerite of Valois, Queen of
Navarre, 49

Marie Louise, Queen of Spain, 70

Markham, George, 95

Markham, William, 128–9, 131, 137–8

Martin, Sir Richard and Lady, 118

Mary I (Tudor): in line of succession
to English throne, 16, 35; death, 20;
at Chatsworth, 37

Mary, Princess: christening, 88;
funeral, 89

Mary, Queen of Scots: death from
porphyria, 9; in custody, 15, 18, 24,
27, 34, 39–40; as first cousin of
Arbella, 15; cares for Margaret
Douglas, 16; accession to Scots
throne, 17; marriage to Darnley,
17–18, 137; abdicates, 18; breach
with Lennox family over Darnley's
death, 22–3; Elizabeth Lennox
spends time with, 22; breach with
Lennox family ends, 24; fondness
for Arbella, 25, 27; porphyria
symptoms and effects, 27, 36–7, 54,
69, 70; hostility to Bess of
Hardwick, 28; Catholicism, 35;
household, 35; role in Babington
plot, 39; condemned to death, 40;
at Wingfield, 43; hysterical attacks,
69; inherits porphyria, 70; body
transferred to Westminster Abbey,
142; Arbella buried beside, 148

Maurice, Count ('Duke of
Guelders'), 85

Mauvissière, Michel de Castelnau,
Seigneur de la, 38

Mayerne, Sir Theodore Turquet de:
records James's symptoms, 36,
69–70, 99–100, 146–7; on summer
heat (1611), 127; notes on Prince
Henry's illness and death, 141–2;
and James's near-death, 144

Melwood Park, South Yorkshire, 95

Mildmay, Sir Walter, 28, 33, 40

Minors, Sergeant, 121, 124

Monson, Sir William, 135–6

Montague, James, 88

More, Sir John, 128, 137, 139

More, Sir Thomas, 38, 145

Morley, Thomas, 47–8
Morton, James Douglas, 4th Earl of, 25
Moundford, Dr Thomas, 117, 119–20, 122–6, 137–8, 146–7, 149

Newcastle, William Cavendish, 1st Duke of, 21
Norden, John, 108
Northampton, Helena, Marchioness of (née Snakenberg), 75–6
Northampton, William Parr, 1st Marquis of, 76, 127
Northumberland, Dorothy, Countess of, 88
Nottingham, Catherine Carey, Countess of: death, 58, 74
Nottingham, Charles Howard, 1st Earl of, 80, 87, 91, 131, 135
Nottingham, Margaret Stuart, Countess of, 91

Ogle, Catherine see Cavendish, Catherine
Oldcoats (house), Derbyshire, 62
Orléans, Henrietta, Duchess of: death from porphyria, 70
Ostend, 133, 135
Overbury, Sir Thomas, 143, 147
Owen, Richard, 73
Oxborough Hall, Norfolk, 28

Paddy, Sir William, 147
Paget family, 35
Palmer, Dr Richard, 143–5, 147
Parry, Sir Thomas, 94, 107–8, 114, 116, 147, 149
Parsons, Father Robert ('Richard Dolman'), 35–6, 48
Paulet, Sir Amyas, 39–40
Philip II, King of Spain, 38, 48
Pierrepoint family, 36
Pierrepoint, Frances, Lady (née Cavendish; Bess of Hardwick's daughter), 21, 27
Pierrepoint, Gervase, 35
Pierrepoint, Sir Henry, 21, 27
porphyria: claims royal victims, 9, 30, 70; symptoms and effects, 27, 35–6, 54, 62, 69–70, 74, 141; hereditary nature, 70

Quarndon Manor, near Loughborough, 95

Raleigh, Elizabeth, Lady (née Throgmorton), 50
Raleigh, Sir Walter, 41, 50, 80–1
Reeves, Edward, 106–7, 109, 129, 143–4, 149
Rimmington, Dr C., 69
Rivers, Father Anthony, 55
Rochester, Robert Carr, Viscount (later Earl of Somerset), 127
Rodney, Edward: and Arbella–William marriage, 105–6; Hertford mistrusts, 105; summoned by Privy Council, 108; carries messages between Arbella and William in prison, 111; signs discharge document for Arbella, 118; in Arbella–William escape plot and attempt, 127–32; in Bruges with William Seymour, 139
Röhl, John, Martin Warner and David Hunt: Purple Secret, 69

Royston, Hertfordshire, 84, 87, 114, 118, 122

Rufford, 22, 95

Ruthven, William, 4th Baron (*later* 1st Earl of Gowrie), 25

Rutland, Roger Manners, 5th Earl of, 115

Sadler, Sir Ralph, 39

St Paul, Sir George, 95

Saintlow, Sir William (Bess of Hardwick's third husband), 20–1

Salisbury, Sir Robert Cecil, 1st Earl of: and Arbella's proposed marriage to Edward Seymour, 58–9; correspondence with Bess on Arbella's behaviour, 61–2, 66, 74; and James's succession to Elizabeth, 74; letters from Arbella, 76–7; suggests Arbella live at Sheen with Lady Northampton, 76; complains of Woodstock accommodation, 79; gives New Year present to Arbella, 82; letter from 7th Earl of Shrewsbury on Arbella's health, 87; negotiates with James for Arbella's right to sell wine in Ireland, 97; letter from Dunfermline on Arbella's betrothal, 104; letter from Hertford, 114; and Arbella's journey north to Durham, 121; and capture of escaping Arbella, 136–7; instructs Trumbull to observe William Seymour in Bruges, 139; death from cancer, 140–1

Sessa, Duke of, 48

Settrington, 22

Seymour, Arbella (William's daughter by Frances), 149

Seymour, Edward (Earl of Hertford's son) *see* Beauchamp, Baron

Seymour, Edward (Lord Beauchamp's son; *later* Baron Beauchamp): Arbella's plan to marry, 55–9; assumes title, 140

Seymour, Frances (*née* Devereux; William's second wife), 149

Seymour, Francis (William's younger brother; *later* Baron Seymour of Trowbridge), 111, 114, 130, 136

Seymour, Jane *see* Jane Seymour, Queen of Henry VIII

Seymour, Lord Thomas, 56

Seymour, William (2nd Duke of Somerset): marriage to Arbella, 9, 105–7, 110; relations with Arbella, 93, 95, 98, 100; arrested, 100–1; betrothal to Arbella, 100, 103–4; makes submission to James on betrothal, 101–3; imprisoned in Tower after marriage, 107–8, 113–14; correspondence with Arbella during detention, 113; and Arbella's stay at Highgate, 118; escape to France, 127–33, 135; reaches Ostend, 133, 135; travels to Bruges, 139; letter to James asking pardon for marriage, 140, 146; final gift from Arbella, 145; moves to Paris, 145; offers no help to Arbella during imprisonment, 145–6; return home and later life, 148; rumoured son by Arbella, 149

Sheen, 76–7; Abbey of, 19

Sheffield Lodge, 27, 34, 36, 87, 91, 94–6

Shrewsbury, Elizabeth Talbot, Countess of (Bess of Hardwick): effect on Arbella, 15; background and marriages, 19–21; inherits from husbands, 19–20, 84; at Queen Elizabeth's court, 20–1; appearance, 21; children's marriages, 21–2; houses, 27, 34, 37–8; and Arbella's upbringing, 28; Mary Queen of Scots' hostility to, 28; and death of daughter Elizabeth, 31; on Arbella's financial situation and education, 32–4; custodial responsibilities for Mary Queen of Scots, 34; marriage difficulties with George, 34–5, 38–9; rift with son Henry, 35, 39, 63, 73–4; and Arbella's spoilt behaviour, 43; bequests to Arbella, 44; treats Arbella more harshly, 44, 46; Burghley warns of plots involving Arbella, 46; life at Hardwick Hall, 53–4; custody of Arbella at Hardwick Hall, 54–5, 59, 63–6; and Arbella's plan to marry Edward Seymour, 58–9; on Arbella's health and mental instability, 61–4; obstructs Arbella's escape attempt from Hardwick, 73–4; will excludes son Henry and Arbella, 74; family rows, 82–4; illness, 88; letter from James, 88; death and funeral, 93; leaves money bequest to Arbella, 93

Shrewsbury, George Talbot, 6th Earl of (Bess's husband): as custodian of Mary Queen of Scots, 15, 18, 24, 34–5, 39; marriage to Bess, 20–1; letters to Burghley, 23–4; marriage difficulties, 34–5, 38–40; dispute with stepsons over land and property, 38–9; as Chief Commissioner for Mary Queen of Scots's trial and execution, 40; anxiety over Arbella as trouble-bringer, 44; invites James to stay at Worksop, 75; death, 76

Shrewsbury, Gilbert Talbot, 7th Earl of: marriage to Bess's daughter Mary, 21; Arbella visits as child, 27; letter to Burghley, 31; devotion to Arbella, 34; sees Mary Queen of Scots' execution, 40; Arbella stays with, 49, 87; Arbella's breach with, 50, 59; as Lord Justice of Eyre, 77; letters from Arbella, 78, 80–1, 85, 94; debts, 84; Arbella helps resolve case against Bess, 85; sends venison pasties to Arbella, 93–4; letter from Arbella on situation of servants, 108–9; signs warrant for Arbella's committal to Durham, 117; and Arbella's ill health on journey to Durham, 119–20; and wife Mary's imprisonment, 138

Shrewsbury, Mary Talbot, Countess of (née Cavendish; 7th Earl's wife): marriage, 21; as godmother to Arbella, 24; Arbella visits, 27; Campion stays with, 36; presents Arbella to Queen Elizabeth, 40; and Catholic plot to kidnap Arbella, 45; Arbella stays with, 49, 87; Arbella's breach with, 50, 58–9; leaves Arbella's letter unanswered, 58–9; with Arbella at Hardwick,

65–6; James invites to Greenwich with Arbella, 76; letters from Arbella, 80–2, 85; plans Arbella's escape, 119, 123, 127–8; attempts to obtain pardon for Arbella, 127; imprisoned in Tower, 137–8, 144, 147, 149; trial and sentence, 140; and Arbella's death, 147; denies knowledge of Arbella's son, 149

Sinclair, Sir Andrew, 90–1

Skinner, Lady, 95

Skipwith, Sir William, 95

Smallwood (estate), Cheshire, 35, 43

Smith, Samuel, 113, 119, 147

Somerset, Anne, Duchess of (Edward Hertford's mother), 55

Sophia, Princess: birth and death, 90

Spanish Armada, 43

Spanish Plot *see* Main, or Spanish Plot

Stafford, Lady Dorothy, 49

Stanhope, Sir John, 59, 63, 66

Stanley, Sir William, 45

Stapleton, Henry, 73–4

Stark, John, 73–4

Stark, Matthew, 74

Starkey, John, 54–5, 59, 68

Stewart, Sir William, 77

Strickland, Agnes, 30

Stuart, Lady Arbella: death from porphyria, 9, 37, 146–7; marriage to William Seymour, 9, 105–7, 110; birth and genealogy, 15, 24; in line of succession to English throne, 15–16, 28, 30, 48–9, 75, 147; disinherited of title by James, 25, 30; health problems and effects of porphyria on, 27, 50, 54, 62, 69–71, 74, 80, 87, 93–5, 99, 113, 117–22, 124–6, 138, 143, 146; embroidering, 28; spoilt as child, 28, 38, 43; grandmother's jewels bequeathed to but stolen, 29–31, 44, 81; allowance from Queen Elizabeth, 31–4, 76; and mother's death, 31, 33; childhood engagement to Lord Denbigh, 38; education and learning, 38–9, 44, 82; marriage prospects, 38, 44–5, 48, 55–7; and execution of Mary Queen of Scots, 40; languages, 40–1, 44, 82, 90; Queen Elizabeth invites to dine, 40–1; friendship with Burghley, 41; deprived of estates, 43; falls out of Queen Elizabeth's favour, 43; portrait as child (aged 13), 43; in grandmother Bess's will, 44; suffers under grandmother Bess, 44, 46, 59, 64–6; Catholic kidnap plots, 45–7; exchanges gifts with Queen Elizabeth, 49; attachment to Earl of Essex, 50–1, 54, 67–9; fall from grace and banishment, 50, 69; confined in Hardwick Hall, 53–9, 69; mental instability, 54, 58–9, 61–5, 67, 69, 71, 80, 110, 143–4; plan to marry Edward Seymour, 57–8; Brounker questions, 58–9, 62–3; letters to Brounker, 64–8, 73, 76, 80; growing hatred of grandmother Bess, 69; attempts to escape from Hardwick, 73–4; excluded from Bess's will, 74; moved to Wrest House, 74–5; not interested in succeeding to throne, 75; refuses to attend Elizabeth's funeral, 75; financial difficulties, 76, 78, 87, 93–4, 97; first meets James, 76; letters to Cecil, 76–7; lives at Sheen, 76–7; Anne of Denmark's friendship with, 77, 79, 84; at James's court, 77–9, 81–2, 84, 88–9; receives pension and allowance from James, 78, 85, 98, 138; plots to place on English throne, 79–81; eye problems, 82; intercedes in family disagreements, 83, 88; as Queen's Carver, 84; hunting, 85; suitors, 85, 93; receives patent from James for peerage, 87–8; friendship with Prince Henry, 89; letter and gift to Christian IV of Denmark, 90–1; performs in masques, 93, 95, 105; relations with William Seymour, 93, 95, 98, 100; and Bess's death, 94; makes royal progress (1608), 95–6; monopoly on selling wine in Ireland, 97, 103; arrested and released (1609), 98; James grants permission to marry a loyal subject, 98, 100; loses favour with James, 99–100; betrothal to William Seymour, 100–4; rearrested after betrothal (1610), 100–1; under house arrest after marriage, 107–10; petitions James and Anne during house arrest, 109–11, 114; correspondence with William during detention, 113; petitions Lord Chief Justices, 114–15; James banishes to Durham, 115–18, 122–4; journey north, 117–22; rests in Barnet, 117–19, 121, 123–7; petitions Council on health grounds, 121; plans escape to France, 123, 127–8; pleads with James for time to recover, 124–5; makes escape, 128–32; intercepted and returned to England, 135–6; imprisoned in Tower, 137, 143–5; last known letter to James pleads for pity, 144; second escape plot frustrated, 144; final illness and death, 146–7; post-mortem report on, 146–7; rumoured interest in converting to Catholicism, 146; embalmed and buried, 148; rumoured son by William, 149

Stuart, Esmé, *see* Lennox, 1st Duke of

Suffolk, Frances Grey, Duchess of, 19

Suffolk, Katherine, Duchess of, 22, 82

Suffolk, Mary, Duchess of, 16

Suffolk, Thomas Howard, 1st Earl of, 132

Sully, Maximilien de Bethune, Duc de, 49

Talbot, Edward (Arbella's cousin), 61

Talbot, Mrs Edward, 61

Talbot, Elizabeth *see* Kent, Countess of

Talbot, Francis: death, 35

Talbot, Gilbert *see* Shrewsbury, 7th Earl of

Talbot, Grace *see* Cavendish, Grace

Talbot, Mary *see* Shrewsbury, Mary, Countess of

Taxis, Don Juan de, 78

Tetbury Castle, Staffordshire, 37, 39

Tethy's Festival (masque), 105

Theobalds (house), Hertfordshire, 93
Toddington, Bedfordshire, 95
Trumbull, William, 100, 139
Tydder, Owen, 57–8

Ulric, Duke of Holstein, 78, 85, 88

Vaughan, Charles, 18
Victoria, Queen, 70
Victoria, Crown Princess (*later*
  Empress) of Germany, 70

Waad, Sir William, 108, 143
Walsingham, Ethelred, Lady, 82
Walsingham, Sir Francis, 28, 32, 34,
  39
Walton Hall, near Chesterfield, 95
Watson, Father, 79
Webster, Thomas, 127
Winchester, 81
Wingfield (house), Derbyshire, 27,
  43, 95
Winwood, Sir Ralph, 128, 131, 137,
  149
Wolsey, Thomas, Cardinal, 19
Woodstock, Oxfordshire, 79, 93
Worcester, Edward Somerset, 4th
  Earl of, 84, 87
Wrest House, Bedfordshire, 74–6, 96

Yelverton, Sir Christopher, 95, 138
Young, Father, 45